advancing learning, changing lives

Edexcel GCSE
History
Controlled Assessment
CA5 Vietnam 1960–75

Rob Bircher and Steve May
Series editor: Angela Leonard

A PEARSON COMPANY

Introduction

This unit is about the Vietnam War, one of the longest and most controversial wars in modern history. This war continues to raise issues and questions that are still researched and analysed by historians, filmmakers, novelists and anybody else who is interested in the basic question: why do countries and human beings engage in war?

You will see why a large and powerful 'superpower' became involved in a conflict that started out as a civil war in a much smaller and less powerful country. You will consider the different types of military strategy used by both sides in this conflict and make judgements about how successful those methods were.

Modern warfare impacts not only on the combatants but also on civilians, and you will see why this aspect became such a controversial part of the conflict. You will also see why both sides found it such a difficult conflict to win, and the part that anti-war protest played in the final outcome.

You are about to research and make judgements about one of the most fascinating and horrific wars in recent history.

Part A of this book covers:

- the reasons for US involvement in Vietnam

- the nature of the conflict and reasons for US defeat

- the impact of the war on civilians and the military, in the USA and in North and South Vietnam

- the growth of protest in the USA and the end of the conflict.

For your controlled assessment in this unit, you will learn how to carry out an enquiry (Part A) and how to analyse and evaluate representations of history (Part B). Later sections of this book cover the skills you will need to be successful in unit 4.

Your Part A enquiry will focus in detail on one key question. In Part B you will focus on representations of history: how to analyse, compare and evaluate different views of the growth of protest.

Contents

Vietnam 1960-75

Part A Carry out a historical enquiry

A1 The reasons for US involvement in Vietnam

4

Learning outcomes

By the end of this topic, you should be able to:

• explain why Vietnam became a country in conflict

• explain why the USA became involved in Vietnam

• make judgements about the importance of the domino theory.

Map of South East Asia. Up until the Second World War, Vietnam, Laos and Cambodia were part of French Indochina.

In March 1965 the US President, Lyndon Baines Johnson, gave the order to send 3,500 marines to South Vietnam. By June of that year that had increased to 82,000. He also instructed the air force to start bombing North Vietnam. This was regarded as a significant escalation of US involvement in Vietnam, which, up to this point, had been based upon sending economic assistance and military 'advisers'. To understand why the USA got involved in Vietnam, we need to find out more about Vietnam's history.

• For centuries, Vietnam was divided into two main parts, the North and the South. There were many wars between the two.

• At the start of the nineteenth century, a leader called Gia Long led a rebellion against Chinese invaders and united the country. He called the country Vietnam.

• Vietnam was not independent for long. Soon the French took control. Vietnam became part of France's overseas empire.

• Vietnam was split up again and, together with its neighbours Laos and Cambodia, became part of a colony called French Indochina.

• During the Second World War, Japan took control of Vietnam. It stripped the country of food. Hundreds of thousands of Vietnamese starved to death.

• When Japan was defeated, the French returned but North Vietnam was determined to fight for independence.

• Ho Chi Minh led the **Vietminh** against the French, fighting for an independent Vietnam. Ho Chi Minh was a communist and wanted Vietnam to be communist.

• French forces were defeated at the battle of Dien Bien Phu in 1954.

• The country was divided into North and South Vietnam at the Geneva Conference in 1954.

Vietnam after the Geneva Conference of 1954.

The USA and Vietnam

After the Second World War, US leaders felt they had to do everything they could to stop the spread of **communism**. The USSR had taken huge parts of Europe as it defeated the Nazis. Then China also became a communist state. China and the USSR wanted other countries to become communist. If that happened, the USA would lose its powerful position as 'the leader of the free world'.

Vietnam was an interesting case:

* Ho Chi Minh was a communist with strong links to China. He wanted a communist Vietnam.
* Ho Chi Minh was fighting for freedom from France as the Americans had once fought for independence from the British Empire.

At first the USA supported Ho Chi Minh against the French; then the USA supported the French, giving them huge amounts of money for their fight against communism.

The battle of Dien Bien Phu

The French thought they could beat Ho Chi Minh's forces, the Vietminh, with superior military skills and technology. They completely underestimated the Vietminh. This is why the French lost the battle of Dien Bien Phu in 1954. The French set up a massive camp around the village of Dien Bien Phu, hoping to lure the Vietminh out of the jungle and into an open fight. The Vietminh did come, but instead of marching straight into battle they dug trenches and tunnels so they could get close to the French while still being protected. Vietminh soldiers kept arriving from all over Vietnam. By the time the battle began there were 70,000 Vietminh surrounding the village – five times as many as the French. For 56 days the Vietminh pushed the French back until they occupied only a very small part of the village. The French surrendered on 7 May 1954 and announced that France wished to withdraw from Vietnam.

Communism: a system of organising society so that all property belongs to the community in general and not to individuals. Everything is controlled by the state and a single political party.

Vietminh: a national liberation movement formed to fight against French and Japanese control of Vietnam.

Activities

1. Imagine you lived in a country ruled by another power. Would you want to fight for your nation's freedom or would you just get on with life as best you could? Explain why.

2. The USA switched from supporting Ho Chi Minh to supporting his enemy, France. Explain why the USA did this. How do you think Ho Chi Minh felt about the USA after this happened?

3. Research the military strategies used by the Vietminh in the war against the French. What lessons could the USA have learnt from this conflict about a conventional army (the French) fighting a 'guerrilla' army (the Vietminh)?

The Geneva Conference (May–July 1954)

After the battle of Dien Bien Phu, representatives from the USA, USSR, Britain, France, China and Vietnam met in Geneva, Switzerland. Their aim was to settle the problem of Vietnam.

- The Vietminh wanted early elections. Having defeated the French, they were sure the Vietnamese people would elect them to form a communist government.
- The USA, Britain and France wanted elections delayed, as they thought the Vietnamese people needed time to consider the type of government they wanted and the type of country they wanted Vietnam to be.

The result of the conference was the Geneva Agreement:

- Vietnam would be divided (temporarily) into North and South (see the map on page 5).
- North Vietnam would be ruled by Ho Chi Minh.
- South Vietnam would be ruled by Ngo Dinh Diem (an anti-communist).
- French troops would fully withdraw from Vietnam.
- The Vietminh would withdraw from South Vietnam.
- The Vietnamese could freely choose to live in the North or the South.
- A general election, for the whole of Vietnam, would be held before July 1956, under the supervision of an international commission.

The domino theory

Ho Chi Minh was sure he would win the election – and so was the USA. If that happened, then Vietnam would become another communist country. The US leaders were very worried that Vietnam would be just the start of a chain of communist take-overs in the whole region. If Vietnam became communist, then it might topple a whole row of countries. This theory was called the 'domino theory'.

The domino theory

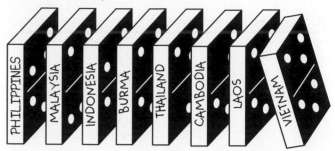

To some people this theory was convincing – it had happened before:

- In the 1930s none of the powerful nations had stood up to Hitler. First the Nazis took control of Austria, then Czechoslovakia, then part of Poland, Denmark, Norway, Luxembourg, the Netherlands, Belgium and France.
- From 1945 to 1948 the USSR had spread and established communism in the states of Eastern Europe.

However, some people were not convinced:

- If Vietnam became communist it was not automatically the case that Laos and Cambodia would become communist.
- There was little evidence at the time to support the idea that places like Thailand, Burma, Indonesia, Malaysia and the Philippines would become communist.

Activity

4. How convincing is the domino theory to you? Do you think Ho Chi Minh would have agreed with it?

Follow up your enquiry

What was the importance of the domino theory?
- Think about its effect on US actions.
- Find evidence from other resources, for example books and websites, to support your opinion.

The Diem government

US President Eisenhower was determined not to let communism spread into South Vietnam. His strategy was to build up South Vietnam so it was strong enough to stand against the North. The USA made sure the newly created Republic of Vietnam (South Vietnam) was led by someone who was strongly anti-communist. This was Ngo Dinh Diem.

Eisenhower decided to send military 'advisers' to support Diem. These advisers were to help Diem to train a South Vietnamese army. The USA also started a propaganda campaign against North Vietnam. It claimed that Vietminh and Chinese communists had entered South Vietnam and were killing innocent civilians.

Also, the North Vietnamese government was accused of killing thousands of Vietnamese, living in the North, who were said to be political opponents of communism. The USA had started a 'psychological war' against communism in Vietnam.

Unfortunately for the USA, Diem ran a corrupt government and was not a popular leader in the South.

Activities

5. In 1954 the USA needed a leader to defend South Vietnam against communism. Imagine you are responsible for drawing up a job description for the ideal candidate for the job. What would be on your list? Here are some starting points:

- the candidate needs to appeal to the public: should have a lot in common with voters
- the candidate should be anti-communist and a supporter of the USA
- the leader will represent democracy and freedom
- most Vietnamese are poor farmers – someone who gave them more land would make them very happy
- there are plenty of Vietminh left in the country – is a strong hand needed to control them?

6. How does Ngo Dinh Diem rate against your ideal candidate list?

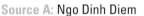

Source A: Ngo Dinh Diem

His election as president was a sham – the vote was rigged. Diem claimed 605,000 votes in Saigon (the capital of South Vietnam), but only 450,000 people were actually allowed to vote.

Diem was a rich Catholic, unlike most Vietnamese, who were mostly poor and Buddhist. He supported rich landowners and persecuted Buddhists.

While Ho Chi Minh gave out land to poor farmers, Diem let rich landowners raise rents so their peasant farmers had to work harder than ever.

Diem hunted down Vietminh supporters and executed them if they did not support him.

Diem gave important official positions to his relatives and friends.

With the backing of the USA, he allowed the election date deadline set by the Geneva Conference (before July 1956) to pass and refused to allow any election to do with the reunification of Vietnam.

The National Liberation Front and civil war, 1959

Vietminh supporters in South Vietnam started the National Liberation Front (**NLF**) to fight against Diem's government and for Ho Chi Minh's united Vietnam. Diem called them the **Viet Cong**, which means 'Vietnamese communist'. The US government also used this term rather than Vietminh. That term was associated with patriotism and nationalism but Viet Cong seemed simple – Vietnamese communists = bad guys. Most commentators still use this term today.

Diem told the USA that he needed many more troops to defend South Vietnam against Viet Cong attacks. It is estimated that approximately 12,000 South Vietnamese government officials were assassinated by the Viet Cong in the first few years of the civil war. In October 1957, US bases in South Vietnam were attacked.

The Viet Cong's aim was to overthrow what they saw as a corrupt and unfair government that Diem (and the USA) had created, and to reunite Vietnam (as the Geneva Agreement had proposed). The Viet Cong thought communism was the best political solution for all of Vietnam. Many of those who joined the Viet Cong were poor, but professional people like teachers and doctors also joined. Peasants and workers (whether they were communist sympathisers or not) supported the organisation, sometimes because the Viet Cong forced them to.

Source B: John F. Kennedy giving his inaugural speech as President of the United States, January 1961.

President John F. Kennedy and Vietnam

When John F. Kennedy became president in January 1961, he spoke of a 'New Frontier' for the USA. For Americans he promised peace, freedom, civil rights and improved living conditions. However, he also spoke about the USA's place in the world. Kennedy had inherited many problems, both at home and abroad, that were complex and not easy to solve.

On the one hand Kennedy wanted the USA, and the world, to think he was tough on communism. But on the other hand he realised that direct military action against communism would be terribly dangerous because the USSR had nuclear weapons that could reach the USA.

This difficult balancing act applied to Vietnam, too. One of his first actions as president was to agree to increase the number of military advisers training the South Vietnamese Army (now known as the Army of the Republic of Vietnam: **ARVN**). There were 16,000 'advisers' in Vietnam by 1963 – so many that it was hard to see them just as 'advisers' any more. But Kennedy was not keen to send US combat troops to Vietnam. That would be getting the USA very heavily involved indeed.

Activities

7. Summarise the factors that led to increased US involvement in the problems of Vietnam in the 1950s. Create a table with the headings:
   - The defeat of the French
   - The domino theory
   - The weakness of Diem's government
   - The actions of the North Vietnamese government.

   Decide which factor you think was the most important.

8. Find out more about the roles and responsibilities of US military 'advisers' in Vietnam. Was sending in thousands of 'advisers' really the same as sending in US troops, or not?

Source C: An aerial photograph of a strategic hamlet, showing a group of houses surrounded by barricades.

Source C: An aerial photograph of a strategic hamlet, showing a group of houses surrounded by barricades.

NLF: National Liberation Front – North Vietnamese supporters in South Vietnam.

Viet Cong: The US and South Vietnamese governments' term for NLF fighters.

ARVN: Army of the Republic of Vietnam – South Vietnamese Army.

NVA: North Vietnamese Army.

Strategic hamlets

Kennedy inherited a very unpopular policy in South Vietnam called the 'strategic hamlets' approach. This had started in 1960, led by Diem's government and the US Central Intelligence Agency (CIA), and was designed to stop the Viet Cong winning over South Vietnamese villages.

If a village was seen to be in danger of Viet Cong 'influence', the villagers were 'relocated' to an 'agroville' or fortified camp, with enclosed ditches, barbed wire fences or sharp bamboo fences. Each of these new villages or 'strategic hamlets' was guarded by local non-communists. Diem and the USA presented this policy as villagers helping and defending themselves.

However, it was difficult to decide which villagers might support the Viet Cong and which did not. Every time ARVN soldiers and US advisers relocated a village (more often than not against residents' wishes), they had no idea if it contained Viet Cong supporters. Equally, as they relocated the village, they had no idea if they were really moving it away from Viet Cong control or moving Viet Cong influence to a new area. Realistically, the South Vietnamese government and the USA had no way of knowing if the policy was working. To make matters worse, relocated peasants were forced to pay for the relocation and the rebuilding of their homes.

The strategic hamlet policy was supposed to 'win the hearts and the minds' of the South Vietnamese people towards Diem's government and the USA. Instead, for many South Vietnamese peasants it was no different from living in a form of prison.

Activities

9. The strategic hamlets approach was designed to 'win hearts and minds'. In pairs, take on the role of advisers to the US president. One of you should be a military adviser explaining why the policy is a good idea and what it will achieve. The other adviser should explain the problems it is causing and what the effects are on support for Diem's regime.

10. Kennedy denied that combat troops were involved in Vietnam, but US jet pilots were bombing Viet Cong positions in South Vietnam and US helicopter pilots were carrying ARVN troops to areas controlled by the Viet Cong. Why do you think he did not want this to be made public?

The overthrow of Diem and his government

From late 1961 it is believed that Kennedy was torn between conflicting advice on both the military and political situation in South Vietnam. Was the US military commitment in South Vietnam really working? Was Diem's government really in control of the situation in South Vietnam? He was not sure. The main US military adviser to the South Vietnamese Army, Lieutenant Colonel Vann, was convinced that the ARVN commanders were making a mess of the situation.

One thing did seem increasingly clear: Diem was not effective at ruling South Vietnam or dealing with the increasing problem of the Viet Cong. Diem could not unite Vietnam against communism (he was not even succeeding in South Vietnam). Kennedy knew that there had been several attempts from within South Vietnam to remove Diem, but he had always instructed the US advisers and CIA to protect Diem. But in 1963 Kennedy removed Diem's protection.

Kennedy agreed to a CIA operation that gave a group of South Vietnamese army generals $40,000 to overthrow the Diem government – a **coup**. Although this was not in Kennedy's plans, Diem and his brother were killed by the generals. Kennedy was shocked by what had happened.

Source D: Christine Bragg, *Vietnam, Korea and US Foreign Policy 1945–75*, 2005.

> With the coup, the US now [took on] direct responsibility for the South Vietnamese government, a situation far more dangerous than the one [President] Kennedy had inherited from [President] Eisenhower.

Results Plus
Watch out

Students often confuse the ARVN and the NVA. Remember that NVA = North Vietnamese Army.

Source E: Geoff Stewart, *Ideology, Conflict and Retreat: The USA in Asia 1950–1973*, 2009.

> Kennedy appears to have been unclear [about] what it was necessary to do. He had repeatedly shown a deep reluctance to commit US ground troops and talked the day before he died of setting up a study group to examine every option, 'including how to get out of there'. Nevertheless, he had stated in public, on many occasions, his commitment to keeping South Vietnam out of communist control... In one of his last press conferences he stated: 'In my opinion, for us to withdraw from that effort, would mean a collapse not only of South Vietnam but South East Asia, so we are going to stay there.'

Source F: Ben Walsh, *GCSE Modern World History*, 2001.

> Diem's regime was... extremely corrupt...The Americans were concerned and frustrated by his actions, but as [US Secretary of State] Dulles said, 'We knew of no one better.' The USA supported Diem's regime with around $1.6 billion in the 1950s. Diem was overthrown by his own army leaders in November 1963, but the governments that followed were equally corrupt. Even so, they also received massive US support.

Activity

11. Study Sources D–F and use them to answer the following questions:
- If the US leaders knew Diem was so corrupt and ineffective, why did they support him?
- What were the consequences of the coup against Diem?
- Was Kennedy determined to defend South Vietnam against communism?

Coup: a sudden overthrow of an existing government and seizure of political power, often carried out by the army.

President Lyndon Baines Johnson

After Kennedy was assassinated in 1963, Johnson took over as president. He had been Kennedy's vice-president. President Johnson immediately introduced the policy of 'Great Society', which promised economic and social improvement for all Americans. However, he could not avoid the situation in Vietnam.

Source G: From a speech made by President Johnson in 1964.

> If we quit Vietnam, tomorrow we'll be fighting in Hawaii and next week we'll have to fight in San Francisco.

The Joint Chiefs of Staff (USA key military personnel) advised Johnson that US combat troops were now needed in South Vietnam. Military advisers were not enough. By 1963 the Viet Cong numbered 23,000. By the end of 1964 estimates suggested this had risen to 60,000. While most of the new Viet Cong recruits came from the South, some were from the North Vietnamese army (**NVA**).

Johnson told his US military chiefs that he would do all he could to prevent a Viet Cong victory in South Vietnam. However, like Kennedy, he was concerned about US public opinion if he started to send US combat troops to South Vietnam. The military chiefs convinced him that if he bombed North Vietnam he might cut off supplies to the Viet Cong along the Ho Chi Minh Trail. But Johnson realised that convincing the US public and world opinion that bombing North Vietnam was justified could be difficult. He was also worried that an unprovoked attack would bring China into the conflict, which the USA was very keen to avoid.

The Ho Chi Minh Trail

The Ho Chi Minh Trail kept the Viet Cong supplied with soldiers, weapons and supplies. The Trail was a supply route which stretched along the border with Laos and Cambodia and re-entered South Vietnam above Saigon (see map opposite). The Trail wasn't just one road or path; it was a very complex network of tracks. Although trucks were used to ferry resources on some parts of the Trail, vast amounts of supplies were transported on foot by peasant farmers, in return for generous payments (in rice) by North Vietnam.

Activities

12. Read Source G carefully. What is the link between Johnson's words and the domino theory?

13. Explain why Johnson was concerned about public opinion in the USA and the world. Why would anyone care if he bombed North Vietnam?

14. Which of the following sources would be best for researching what US presidents Kennedy and Johnson really felt about the situation in Vietnam: personal diaries, TV interviews, Wikipedia, books about them by close friends and colleagues? Explain your answer.

A map of the Ho Chi Minh Trail.

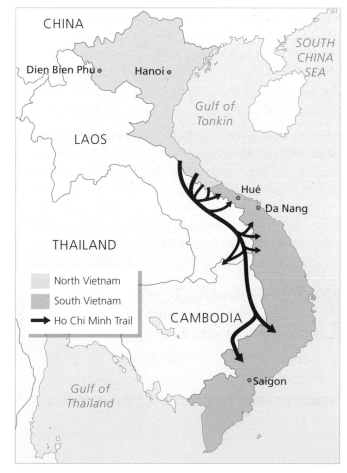

The Gulf of Tonkin incident

Even though Johnson expressed personal doubts about the conflict in South Vietnam, when the opportunity came to escalate the war, he seized it. This happened in the Gulf of Tonkin incident.

The Gulf of Tonkin, in North Vietnam, was a busy waterway. The US and South Vietnamese forces carried out several secret missions there against the North Vietnamese. For example, OPLAN 34A, a sabotage and intelligence-gathering mission, was carried out by South Vietnamese forces, the CIA and US Special Forces all working together.

On the night of 31 July 1964, commandos of the South Vietnamese army attacked a North Vietnamese radar station in the Gulf of Tonkin. A US warship, the *USS Maddox*, was involved in monitoring the North Vietnamese radar stations. On 2 August 1964, North Vietnamese torpedo boats attacked the US warship – it was hit by a torpedo which did not explode. The *USS Maddox* fired on the torpedo boats and US fighter planes sank one of them and damaged two more.

On 4 August 1964 the *USS Maddox* and the *USS Turner Joy* reported that they had been fired upon and attacked by torpedo boats. It was later revealed that no sailor on board the ships, or jet fighter pilots in the air, saw any evidence of this second attack. But in the USA it was reported without doubt that US ships had been attacked again. As a consequence, Johnson ordered the air force to attack North Vietnamese gunboat bases, and many were destroyed.

Source H: Television address by President Johnson to the US public on the night of 4 August 1964.

> Repeated acts of violence against the armed forces of the United States must be met not only with alert defence, but with positive reply. That reply is being given as I speak to you tonight.

The USA was outraged by what was reported as an unprovoked attack by North Vietnam. Johnson seized his chance and proposed the 'Gulf of Tonkin Resolution'. This gave the president the power to defend US forces and South Vietnam in whatever

way he thought best. The US Congress believed that the second attack had taken place, and agreed.

Having taken over as US President after Kennedy's assassination in 1963, in November 1964 Johnson was elected in a 'landslide' victory over his opponent Barry Goldwater. Goldwater had called for an escalation of the war against North Vietnam and suggested that combat troops should be sent to Vietnam. Johnson appeared to want a more peaceful solution and stated that he was unsure about the need to send combat troops. Once he was elected, though, his attitude seemed to change.

Activity

15. Why did the Gulf of Tonkin incident lead to increased US involvement in the Vietnam conflict?

Follow up your enquiry

Research the Gulf of Tonkin in more detail. Make sure your notes cover what happened in the incident, what the Gulf of Tonkin Resolution contained, and what the consequences were for the escalation of US involvement in Vietnam.

Source I: A photograph of the *USS Maddox*, the US warship involved in the Gulf of Tonkin incident.

The Part A skills section of this book (pages 44–53) focuses on the Gulf of Tonkin incident.

Operation Rolling Thunder

Within three months of his election, Johnson approved an operation codenamed 'Rolling Thunder' – regular air attacks on North Vietnam. The aim was to bomb key positions in North Vietnam, in order to cripple its economy and make it difficult for it to supply the Viet Cong. Viet Cong in the South were also regularly bombed. Operation Rolling Thunder was supposed to last for eight weeks, but it lasted for three years: from March 1965 to November 1968. Over one million tons of bombs were dropped on Vietnam.

The new leader of the US military advisers in South Vietnam, General Westmoreland, told Johnson that his current force of 23,000 men was not enough to deal with the Viet Cong threat. On 8 March 1965, 3,500 US marines were sent to South Vietnam to strengthen the US effort.

Source J: A photograph of a US air force bomber during Operation Rolling Thunder.

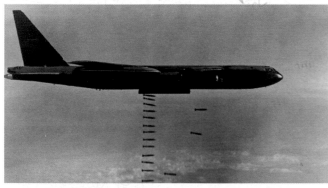

Johnson presented these actions to the US public as necessary, but more importantly, as 'short-term' measures. At this point US opinion polls showed that about 80% of the US public supported these actions.

Activity

16. Plot a graph to show the escalation of the conflict.
   - Put years along the x-axis (horizontal) starting at 1945 and ending at 1968.
   - On the y-axis (vertical) put 'US commitment' – a scale of 0 to 100% would be useful here.
   - For each of the following events, plot where it happened in time and estimate how much it committed the USA to war in Vietnam:
     – 16,000 'advisers' now in Vietnam
     – the assassination of Diem
     – the Gulf of Tonkin incident
     – Operation Rolling Thunder starts
     – 3,500 marines sent to Vietnam.

   You can add in other events too if you like.

Did you know?

US troops often called their enemy in Vietnam 'Charlie'. This was because the term Viet Cong got shortened to the initials V.C., and the letters V.C. in US radio communication were called 'Victor Charlie'.

Your conclusion so far

From this topic, we have seen:
- The Vietnam War had deep roots, including the decision by the USA to prevent South Vietnam from becoming communist.
- The USA became involved in Vietnam in a step-by-step way, each new development making it harder to get out again.
- The domino theory was the basis for US involvement in Vietnam, but Ho Chi Minh's struggle was more about achieving independence than communism.

From what you have learned in this topic, what were the reasons why the USA became more involved in Vietnam by 1965?

To answer this question, create a spider diagram of all the factors in this section that contributed to the USA becoming more involved. Include, for example, the domino theory, the collapse of the Diem regime, underestimating North Vietnam and the Viet Cong.

Consider:
- how the factors link to each other – show this with arrows
- which were the most important factors – mark these in red.

Compare your judgements with those of other people in your group.

A2 The nature of the conflict and reasons for US defeat

Learning outcomes

By the end of this topic, you should be able to:

- explain and evaluate the military methods used by the USA and the ARVN in Vietnam
- explain and evaluate the military methods used by the Viet Cong in Vietnam
- make judgements about why the USA and the South Vietnamese government were unable to win the conflict in Vietnam.

On paper there appeared to be no contest – a mighty military machine against a peasant army. But the US found it very difficult to make headway against the Viet Cong and North Vietnam.

One reason for this was because the different sides to the conflict had different **objectives**. When we think of a traditional war, we tend to imagine two armies facing each other on open ground. The objective is to keep on fighting until the other side is dead, runs away or surrenders. The objectives in the Vietnam War were not like this.

Objective: the overall aim or goal.

Strategy: the plan of action to achieve the objective.

Tactics: the methods and activities used in the plan.

North Vietnam objective

Unification of North and South Vietnam under communist government

Viet Cong objective

Build up support in South Vietnam to help achieve North Vietnam's objective

US objective

Stop communists taking over in South Vietnam

South Vietnam government objective

Keep control over South Vietnam and keep US support

To achieve their objectives, each side developed different **strategies**. Strategies are like long-term plans:

North Vietnam/Viet Cong strategies

1. Convince the people of South Vietnam to get rid of their government
2. Destroy the morale of the ARVN
3. Inflict enough damage on the USA to convince it to withdraw
4. Never give in

South Vietnam government strategies

1. Remove the Viet Cong from villages
2. Defend South Vietnam from invasion
3. Rely on massive amounts of US money

US strategies

1. Force North Vietnam to give up the war
2. Make North Vietnam agree an acceptable solution to the conflict
3. Make sure the USSR or China are not drawn into the conflict
4. Protect South Vietnam while building support among its population

These are fairly simple summaries of the strategies. In reality the strategies were more complex and they also changed over time. But even at this very simple level, you will have noticed that the USA had a major problem: if the USA used too much force it could make the USSR or China move in to defend communist North Vietnam. That could lead to nuclear war. So the USA was in a fight with one hand tied behind its back. Also, the success of the US strategies depended on North Vietnam eventually realising it could never win against US power. But one of the North Vietnamese strategies was 'never give in' – it was confident it knew how to beat its powerful opponent.

To put their strategies into practice, each side developed different **tactics**. Tactics are specific approaches to particular situations. Military methods are mostly about tactics. Tactics rarely stay the same for long: the other side learns to adapt to your tactics and then you need to develop what you do to counter the other side's tactics, and so on. We will look at tactics in more detail over the next few pages.

Source A: A photograph showing three Viet Cong prisoners of war under the control of US soldiers. What differences can you see between the US and Viet Cong troops?

North Vietnam/Viet Cong: tactics based on use of guerrilla warfare
- Build bases of support among the local population
- Avoid open battles with the enemy
- Use the local population to gather intelligence about troop movements
- Use ambushes
- Attack at night
- Withdraw from fights when outnumbered

USA/ARVN: tactics based on use of superior military force
- Bomb North Vietnam into surrendering
- Bomb and cut off supply routes from North Vietnam to the Viet Cong
- Use ground troops to defend bases and cities
- Carry out 'search and destroy' missions on enemy units
- Build trust with the South Vietnamese population

Activities

1. What would have counted as winning the war for the USA? Think about its *objectives* when giving your answer.

2. Over the next 7 pages, consider each of the *tactics* described and evaluate how effective these were in meeting the objectives of the side that used them.

Guerrilla warfare: a type of warfare where a smaller, less well-supplied force uses stealth and hit-and-run tactics to fight a larger force.

US military tactics

US military tactics were designed to do two things: attack North Vietnam and defend South Vietnam.

Attacking North Vietnam: Operation Rolling Thunder

The Gulf of Tonkin Resolution (see page 12) had given President Johnson the opportunity to use the tactic of bombing North Vietnam. This operation was codenamed 'Rolling Thunder' (see page 13).

Between 2 March 1965 and 1 November 1968 North Vietnam was repeatedly bombed by the US air force. The aim was to:

- make the North Vietnamese give up the war and agree to South Vietnam being a separate country
- halt the flow of equipment and men to the Viet Cong in South Vietnam down the Ho Chi Minh trail (see page 11).

By December 1965 over 25,000 bombing missions had been flown and over 32,000 tons of bombs had been dropped on North Vietnam. This was hugely expensive for the USA, and it also cost the lives of many US airmen. By the time Operation Rolling Thunder was stopped (November 1968), 745 US crewmen had been shot down. Those who survived were kept as prisoners of the North Vietnamese.

As time went on the weaknesses of the US tactic of using large-scale bombing to achieve its objectives became clearer:

- The USA had to be careful not to use too much force as this might tip the USSR or China into war to support North Vietnam. So at the start the bombing was carefully controlled – no bombing of major cities, no bombing of airfields and certainly no bombing anywhere near the border with China.
- The USA did not anticipate the determination and resilience of the people of North Vietnam. Despite between 50,000 and 200,000 civilian deaths from the bombing, **morale** remained high. After every bombing mission, thousands of people volunteered to repair the damage. North Vietnam refused to give up.

- Bombing missions were often flown in heavy rain and fog. The US air force was not used to these conditions.
- The North Vietnamese were supported by the USSR, who supplied early warning radar stations.

Source B: CIA document, 1965, about the damage from one air strike in North Vietnam. This document was top secret at the time – what do you think made this information so sensitive?

- Four specific buildings in Vinh Linh town destroyed; headquarters of district administrative committee; state trade office, theatre, and hospital.
- Grade school and two-thirds of houses in area destroyed.
- Barracks of 270th regiment destroyed.

Activity

3. Look back at page 14 and make a numbered list of the US strategies. Then draw up a table like this one and fill in the first row for Operation Rolling Thunder. Some points have been added to get you started. Use a big piece of paper or do this on screen as you will add new rows to the table as you work through this section.

The success of US military tactics

Strategies	Military tactic	Evaluation – how effective?
1 and 3	Operation Rolling Thunder: large-scale bombing of North Vietnam	Not successful – really expensive in both money and lives, but had little impact on North Vietnamese morale because...

Defending South Vietnam

It is easy to start thinking of the US conflict in Vietnam as being like a 'standard' war between countries: the US against the Viet Cong in a struggle for control of territory. But it was not that sort of a war. Remember, this was a **civil war** between North Vietnam and South Vietnam. The USA was there to help an anti-communist South Vietnam survive. The US strategy was to protect South Vietnam while building up support among its population. If the aim had been to prevent a North Vietnamese invasion, maybe all the US forces would have needed to do was to defend the border zone (called the demilitarised zone – DMZ). However, this was not possible because:

- the Viet Cong were already in South Vietnam
- there was not just one border to defend – North Vietnam could get into South Vietnam through Laos and Cambodia.

Civil war: a war between different groups of people within the same state.

Cluster bombs: bombs used by the US military which released hundreds of smaller 'bomblets' over a wide area.

Morale: the belief of a group of people in their shared aims and their ability to work together to achieve it.

The US and the South Vietnamese governments knew that South Vietnam would never survive until they got rid of the Viet Cong from that part of the country. The Viet Cong had a lot of influence on the South Vietnamese people. Until the Viet Cong were removed, it would be impossible to start building South Vietnam as an independent country. You saw on page 9 that one early attempt by the South Vietnamese government to do this was the strategic hamlets approach.

ResultsPlus
Top Tip

Students who do well will focus on the point of their enquiry. For example, to decide how *effective* military tactics were, don't just describe them. Think first about what the tactics were designed to achieve, and then find out how successful they were at this.

US forces tackled the Viet Cong too. The aim was to search for and find Viet Cong forces and then destroy them. This was difficult because the Viet Cong were guerrilla fighters. They did not come out in the open to fight giant battles. They did not look different from local South Vietnamese. They were supported by local people. They hid in the jungle and attacked at night. They had plenty of supplies coming down the Ho Chi Minh trail. So how did the US tackle them?

US air power

The US had the air superiority to bomb North Vietnam – the North Vietnamese or Viet Cong forces could try to shoot down planes and helicopters but they did not have the planes to tackle US airpower directly. The US also developed sophisticated military methods to defend South Vietnam using airpower. Once enemy forces were located they could be attacked from the air with bombs and missiles. US airpower was probably what the Viet Cong and North Vietnamese feared the most.

Cluster bombs

A very effective way of killing or injuring lots of enemy troops was to use **cluster bombs**. Dropped from an aircraft, these bombs exploded in mid-air and released up to 600 smaller bomblets. As these hit the ground they shot out thousands of pieces of metal, killing and injuring over a wide area. Later these types of bombs contained fibreglass fragments. After an explosion these fragments could be inhaled and infect the lungs, as well as cut into skin. It was later revealed that fibreglass was not easily detectable under x-ray.

Follow up your enquiry

The Viet Cong was very good at getting support from the South Vietnamese. This is often described as 'winning the hearts and minds' of the South Vietnamese. The South Vietnamese government and the USA were often very bad at it. Research this key topic further and list reasons for the successes of the Viet Cong and the failures of the US and South Vietnam governments on this strategy.

Napalm

Another way of trying to kill many enemy troops from the air was to use **napalm**. When napalm bombs hit the ground and exploded they released flaming petroleum jelly. This was like a burning hot shower. The jelly would stick to anything and burn it: houses, forest – and human skin. During the Vietnam conflict over 400,000 tons of napalm was dropped by the US air force onto suspected enemy targets. It was also sprayed from US military river boats.

> **Napalm:** gasoline mixed with a paste of chemicals to form a jelly. When ignited, the jelly structure means the burning gasoline sticks to substances (like skin), increasing the damage done by this weapon.

Defoliants

US planes were also used to drop chemicals known as defoliants, which destroyed plants. The Viet Cong were being supplied from the North via the Ho Chi Minh Trail (see page 11) but the US combat troops and ARVN had great difficulty finding out exactly where this route was – it went through different types of terrain: mountains, jungle, dense forest and even rivers. Much of the trail was covered by trees and thick undergrowth. The US decided that if they could not find it on the ground they would use aircraft to spray defoliants over a 'suspected' area of the trail. This would then make it easy to see people moving supplies, and kill them. The best known of the defoliants was Agent Orange. In all, it is estimated that approximately 77 million litres of this acid was sprayed over Vietnam.

However, destroying huge areas of forest cover did not stop the supply of men and supplies down the Ho Chi Minh Trail, and the acid also drifted for miles and destroyed the crops of local people. It is estimated that over 4 million Vietnamese people were exposed to the acid. It also settled on animals and got into water supplies. After the Vietnam conflict was over it was estimated that there had been over 400,000 deaths and cases of disability related to the use of Agent Orange. Also, approximately 500,000 children were born with defects that were linked to the acid. These ranged from deformity of limbs to cancer.

Source C: Napalm sprayed from US military river boats.

Source D: A US plane spraying defoliant.

Problems with air attacks

One problem for the USA with air attacks was that they were not very accurate. Ground troops could radio in an air strike, but it is difficult to drop bombs from a very fast, high-flying plane and have them land exactly where they are supposed to. Sometimes US troops ended up getting bombed by their own side. Sometimes ground troops called in an air strike even though they were not very sure where the enemy actually was. And sometimes the enemy had built underground shelters to hide in.

Another problem with an air attack is that it is indiscriminate: civilians can be hurt as well as enemy troops. Many South Vietnamese civilians, including children, were killed or injured by US air attacks, in addition to the deaths and disabilities caused by napalm and defoliants. These were the very people the US and ARVN forces were supposed to be protecting.

Airmobility

Airmobility was developed in Vietnam. The US used helicopters to move ground troops and equipment quickly into an enemy area, supply them while they were there, and then get them out again. Airmobility needed excellent planning and highly trained troops who had to fight under lots of different conditions. Airmobility was very flexible, rapidly bringing in more troops when needed and taking wounded soldiers to field hospitals much more quickly, saving many lives.

When airmobility was used in air attacks it was very difficult to fight against. Instead of fighting what they thought was a small reconnaissance unit, the Viet Cong and NVA would suddenly find themselves facing a much larger number of ground troops, who would call in air strikes and then attack any survivors.

Source E: Helicopters from the 1st Air Cavalry Division on a search and destroy mission in South Vietnam, January 1967.

Search and destroy missions

Airmobility helped US forces and the ARVN to tackle a major problem: finding the enemy. Even when the Viet Cong and North Vietnamese Army (NVA) were moving large numbers of troops around they were very good at staying under cover. But once large numbers of troops had been spotted, airmobility could get US forces in and fighting very quickly. This military method was called 'search and destroy'.

At first the Viet Cong and NVA found it difficult to counter this tactic, but soon they found ways to bring helicopters down – they were slow moving and vulnerable to rocket attack. Also, as soon as any signs of US forces were detected, the Viet Cong and NVA soldiers would move to another area as fast as they could – often just returning to local villages. They developed the tactic of tricking US troops into ambushes – revealing a small number of their troops while much larger numbers hid, waiting for the helicopters to come in. And the Viet Cong and NVA also developed the tactic of 'hugging' US forces: staying so close to them in combat that the US could not use air strikes because of the risk of hitting their own soldiers.

Source F: A description of a typical search and destroy mission from *The Vietnam War: The Story and Photographs*.

Vietnam was singularly ill-suited for this type of operation. The usual blue-print for a search and destroy mission was to obtain intelligence – which might or might not be reliable. According to the level of enemy activity or presence reported, the Americans sent off what they considered an appropriate unit – anywhere from a platoon to a battalion – to locate the Viet Cong or NVA positions. Then an air and/ or military strike was launched to prepare the way for the helicopters to land with additional troops. Sometimes the effort netted results; more often it did not. Such missions were often ineffective because at the slightest hint of American activity the communist forces slipped away into the jungle or countryside.

Search and destroy in villages

As well as using search and destroy on a large scale to find and fight large numbers of enemy troops on the move or at training bases, US forces and the ARVN also went out on missions to villages to try and find Viet Cong fighters, organisers and supporters. The Viet Cong were very successful at getting local support for their cause, and there was no way South Vietnam could ever stand against North Vietnam while that was happening.

Unfortunately, the methods used in many of these missions only made villagers hate the US forces and the ARVN. Because it was so difficult to tell who was Viet Cong and who was not, the soldiers used intimidation and violence to get information from villagers. If they suspected villagers of hiding VC soldiers or supplies, they might burn down houses or destroy food supplies, even if nothing had been proved. The US troops increasingly referred to these missions as 'Zippo raids', because they set fire to thatched huts with their Zippo lighters.

The US Commander of Military Operations in South Vietnam, General Westmoreland, believed that search and destroy was an effective military strategy. However, it proved difficult to convince the US public that it was successful:

- Search and destroy missions went into enemy territory and then came out, and the enemy just moved back in again – what was the point?
- The US public was used to their soldiers being heroes, not beating up women and children and then burning down their houses.
- Search and destroy did not seem to be reducing the enemy's ability to attack South Vietnam or reducing the level of support it had among South Vietnamese people.

Source G: Picture of a suspected Viet Cong soldier being interrogated by US combat soldiers.

Activity

5. Continue your table from the activity on page 16. Add two more rows: one for search and destroy against troops and one for search and destroy in villages. Complete the Strategies and Evaluation columns for each, as before.

ResultsPlus

Top Tip

Students who can show how factors link together and explain their importance can gain the highest marks in Part A of their controlled assessment.

Viet Cong military methods – guerrilla tactics

When they fought the French in the late 1940s and 1950s, the Vietminh had learned how successful their guerrilla tactics could be against a large, well-equipped conventional army. The Viet Cong applied this lesson against the combined forces of the US military and ARVN.

The Viet Cong:

- tried not to confront their enemy in an all-out, open battle
- attacked their opponents when they were at their weakest, for example after a long march
- attacked when their enemies were resting or in camp
- retreated when the other side attacked.

Effectively, the Viet Cong never fought out in the open and rarely 'face to face'. While this method did not necessarily mean quick success it certainly frustrated their opponents.

The objective of the Viet Cong was not the outright defeat of the ARVN or the US forces so they could take control of South Vietnam. They knew that they just needed to inflict enough damage to make the war so unpopular with the US public that US forces would have to be withdrawn.

They attacked those who supported the South Vietnamese government, and hoped to wear down the morale of the ARVN. The most important objective was to build enough support in South Vietnam to achieve their goal: unification of South Vietnam with North Vietnam.

South Vietnamese: 'winning hearts and minds'

The ordinary South Vietnamese people were caught up in the conflict. Many supported the Viet Cong – either because they believed the Viet Cong were right, because they were friends or relations of the Viet Cong, or because they were forced to.

The Viet Cong treated the South Vietnamese peasants with respect. They helped out in the paddy fields and were courteous to them. In return they got food, places to hide and in some areas increasing support. Many peasants actively supported the Viet Cong by keeping the Ho Chi Minh Trail open. However, the Viet Cong could be ruthless and brutal. Peasants who were known as supporters (or collaborators) of the enemy were terrorised and threatened, and some were killed. Other South Vietnamese people who worked for the South Vietnamese government became targets for the Viet Cong. An estimated 30,000 teachers, police and tax collectors were killed during the conflict by the Viet Cong.

Activity

6. Make a numbered list of the North Vietnam and Viet Cong strategies on page 14. Start a new table like the one below, this time for Viet Cong and NVA military tactics. The first two columns have been started for you.

Viet Cong and NVA military methods

Strategies	Military tactic	Evaluation – how effective?
2 3 4	Use guerrilla warfare methods	
1	Build base of support among local population	

Viet Cong tunnel systems

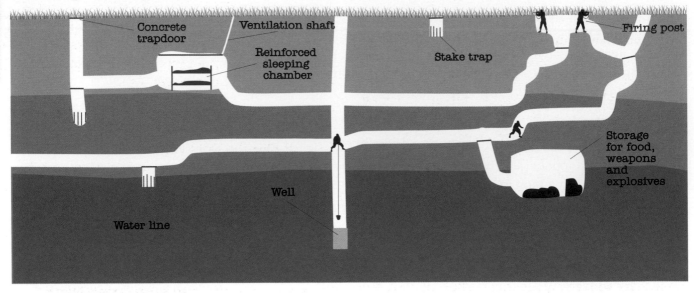

Diagram of Viet Cong tunnel system.

The Viet Cong dug themselves tunnels to provide shelter from bombing and search and destroy missions. The tunnels were mostly in the countryside and jungle, but some were in towns and major cities like Saigon. Having dug them, the Viet Cong sometimes then rigged them with 'booby traps' and left them. Unsuspecting US and ARVN troops entered these tunnels and triggered the explosives, causing many deaths and casualties.

'Booby traps' and mines

The traps the Viet Cong used in their tunnels were also used in the countryside and jungle to catch out the US and ARVN troops. The 'booby traps' and mines were simple to construct and very effective. They meant US and ARVN soldiers had to move slowly and carefully, that they were always frightened and it was psychologically damaging and demoralising for soldiers to see friends blown apart with no enemy in sight.

It has been estimated that 60% of US casualties in the war came from mines and booby traps. One common danger was the 'Bouncing Betty'. This was a type of landmine that would not detonate on the ground, but instead would jump up a few feet before exploding shrapnel at waist level.

Source H: Interview with Vietnam veteran Fred Downs, from the Center for Defense Information website.

I was walking along smoking a cigarette, and I looked at my watch and said, oh, seven forty-five in the morning. And, next thing I knew, I was flying through the air and it was black powder and dirt rushing by me, and I threw my arms up like this, and I realized that something drastic had gone wrong... There was just a jagged bone there. The arm was gone... And, then [my other] arm: I could see both bones in this arm from the wrist to the elbow, because all that was blown away. And, part of my thumb, my hand... I staggered forward and fell down and rolled over on my back... I sort of knew it was a Bouncing Betty... I'd seen a lot of my men get hit and just instinctively knew what it was.

Activity

7. Continue your table from the activity on page 21. Add two new rows: one for tunnel systems and another for booby traps and mines. Complete the Strategies and Evaluation columns.

Stalemate: a situation in which neither side can make progress.

Breaking the stalemate: The Tet Offensive, 1968

Who was winning by 1968?

Overall, the military methods used by both sides produced a **stalemate** effect. The USA had a mighty and highly technological military machine, but against an almost invisible peasant army this could not achieve victory. Even when the USA killed thousands of Viet Cong or NVA troops, as in the first major battle of the war at La Drang Valley (November 1965), it was hard for it to claim victory. As soon as US forces pulled out, their opponents retook the area. The Viet Cong and NVA forces were building support in South Vietnam and the loss of US soldiers was making the war very unpopular with many Americans. But the USA was still there. Maybe the USA needed a catastrophic defeat, like the French at Dien Bien Phu (see page 5), to convince it to leave Vietnam.

What was needed in this conflict was for one side to come out of its 'comfort zone' and aim for all-out victory. Surprisingly, it was the Viet Cong who made this move.

Build-up to the Tet Offensive

During 1967 the Viet Cong launched a series of attacks against US forces. At the time General Westmoreland believed that these attacks were playing into the USA's hands, and it was reported that during them the Viet Cong lost over 90,000 men. However, what was not fully understood at the time by US military chiefs was that these attacks were part of a bigger plan.

On 31 January the Vietnamese celebrated Tet, the Vietnamese New Year. During the evening of 31 January 1968 the Viet Cong launched an attack on over 100 towns and cities in South Vietnam. It was now realised that the earlier attacks that took place during 1967 had been attempts by the Viet Cong to draw US troops away from these targets.

Many historians now consider that the Tet Offensive was a major disaster for the Viet Cong. After this offensive it was largely North Vietnamese fighters who took up the struggle in the South, giving much more control on strategy to the NVA leadership in Hanoi. General Westmoreland also claimed it as a major victory for the US and ARVN forces. But the American public were deeply worried by the news coverage of the offensive. They had been told that the USA was winning the war. If that was true, how on earth could the enemy strike in over 100 South Vietnamese cities and towns – including an attack on the US Embassy in Saigon itself?

Source I: Street fighting in the city of Hué during the Tet Offensive. This beautiful old city was largely destroyed by the US forces as they 'saved' it from the Viet Cong.

Activities

8. Find out about the Siege of Khe Sanh that took place between January and April 1968.

9. Was the Tet Offensive a victory or a failure for the Viet Cong? Which of the following points had positive and which had negative impacts for the Viet Cong?

   - Viet Cong troops entered the grounds of the US Embassy in Saigon and five US marines were killed.
   - The Viet Cong could not take control of the US Embassy in Saigon.
   - The Viet Cong captured Saigon's main radio station for a few hours.
   - Millions of Americans (and people around the world) witnessed battles from this offensive on TV news reports.
   - The Viet Cong attacked the city of Hué and held it for 25 days.
   - In Hué the Viet Cong executed approximately 3,000 Vietnamese suspected of supporting the South Vietnam government.
   - US troop deaths: 1,500.
   - ARVN troop deaths: 2,800.
   - Viet Cong troop deaths: 45,000.
   - Viet Cong troop casualties: 170,000.
   - Many of the Viet Cong deaths were of their most experienced fighters.
   - ARVN troops did not perform well against Viet Cong fighters.
   - The Tet Offensive wiped out most of the Viet Cong's soldiers; after this, new recruits mostly came from North Vietnam.
   - Images of South Vietnamese police executing suspected Viet Cong in the streets of Saigon were seen around the world.
   - The US public saw how Vietnamese civilians were caught up in this war.

10. Go through the two tables you have completed: for the US and ARVN military methods, and the Viet Cong and NVA military methods. On balance, which side had the most effective methods for achieving their objectives? Explain your answer.

11. Does the Tet Offensive show that US military methods were the best because so many Viet Cong were killed, or does it show that US military search and destroy methods were useless because they failed to detect or prevent such a massive Viet Cong build-up?

12. Follow up what happened after the Tet Offensive. Did it prove to be a turning point in the Vietnam War?

Your conclusion so far

From this topic we have seen that:

- The USA's overwhelming military superiority in Vietnam was like having a massive hammer in a room too small to swing it.
- The Viet Cong were very effective at using guerrilla tactics to wear down US and ARVN troops.
- The USA and ARVN were very bad at winning the hearts and minds of the South Vietnamese; the Viet Cong were much better at this.
- The USA's objective was protecting South Vietnam – but for how long?

From what you have learned in this topic, why do you think the USA (supporting the South Vietnamese forces) was not able to secure victory in this conflict? To answer this question, look at these five factors. Which of them do you think are most important in explaining why the USA could not win its war? Explain why.

- The USA could not use full force against North Vietnam because of China and the USSR.
- The US and South Vietnamese governments failed to win the hearts and minds of the South Vietnamese.
- The USA underestimated North Vietnam's determination to win the war.
- Many Americans did not believe the USA should be fighting in Vietnam.
- The USA could not prevent the Viet Cong from being supplied by North Vietnam.

A3 The impact of the war on civilians and the military

Learning outcomes

By the end of this topic, you should be able to:

- understand the impact of the Vietnam War on combatants
- understand the impact of the Vietnam War on civilians
- assess the impact of the Vietnam War on civilians and combatants as a factor that helps explain why the USA did not win this conflict.

What decides the outcome of war is not always the military victories or losses; it is also the effect war has on people. The Vietnam conflict was as much a struggle to 'win hearts and minds' as it was a fight on a battlefield. Let's look at what the USA wanted to achieve:

- It wanted to stop the spread of communism. Its leaders believed the
  US public would support the conflict because it would make them safer from communism.
- The USA would use massive force (bombing) to show the North Vietnamese people there was no point in them supporting Ho Chi Minh's plans for Vietnam.
- The USA would defend the South Vietnamese people so they could build a strong, anti-communist South Vietnam.

This plan depended upon persuading people to think in a particular way, but US leaders completely misread the situation in North Vietnam and South Vietnam. Many Americans lost their belief in why the USA was in the war: not just civilians, but also many soldiers too.

The more frustrating US troops found it to fight the Viet Cong, the more likely they were to take out their frustration on the South Vietnamese villagers they thought were Viet Cong supporters. This brutality made many villagers hate the USA and the South Vietnamese government, which increased support for the Viet Cong. The US public could not understand why US soldiers were dying so far from home for a country that did not seem to want them there. The North Vietnamese grew confident that all they had to do was wait for the US public to make their leaders end the war, and then they could take control of the South easily. The way the war affected people, both combatants and civilians, had a major impact on the outcome of the conflict.

ResultsPlus

Top Tip

Always back up the points you make using accurate information. For example, if you say that one factor leading to US defeat was US public opinion, you could use information from pages 26 and 30–31 to support your point.

ResultsPlus

Watch out

Because the USA did not win, students often assume that the USA was bound to lose this conflict. Take care to explain why the USA was unable to win.

Part A: Carry out a historical enquiry

The impact that the war had on those fighting (combatants) and those not fighting (civilians) formed a terrible downward spiral for the USA, with one factor reinforcing another, pushing the USA toward accepting that it would not be able to do what it had set out to achieve.

The downward spiral: how the events of the war affected US soldiers and public opinion.

The Viet Cong stay strong against US forces

Bombing North Vietnam only makes its civilians more determined to resist the USA

It is hard for US troops to fight the Viet Cong: US troops lose morale, discipline suffers

The Viet Cong are very good at getting support from the South Vietnamese people

North Vietnam sees it is 'winning hearts and minds' in the South

South Vietnamese civilians resent their brutal treatment by US and ARVN forces

The US public is shocked at reports of brutality by US troops

The US public is alarmed by US casualties and asks: is it worth it?

North Vietnam sees the US public turning against the war and so feels it is winning

ResultsPlus
Top Tip

This diagram helps you to show how factors interact – how they work together. You could try redrawing it with new labels to show an upward spiral for North Vietnam.

The impact of the war on the US military

The Vietnam War was not the same experience for all the US military involved in it. But in overall terms the general experience was a very difficult one:

- It was not clear to US soldiers what the war was being fought for.
- It was not clear who the enemy was.
- The enemy was often hidden and 'invisible'. US soldiers died never seeing who shot them or who laid the mine that blew them up.
- Many fighting in the war had not volunteered to go to Vietnam, they had been drafted – conscripted by the government (see below).
- As the war progressed, the anti-war movement grew in the USA and soldiers knew that few people would welcome them back as heroes.
- Vietnam was also a very hostile, alien environment for many US soldiers to be in.

This all had a big impact on military morale. Between 1963 and 1973 over 500,000 cases of desertion were recorded. There was also a big rise in cases where soldiers refused to obey orders.

Next, let's look at three particular ways in which the war had an impact on the US military.

'Cherries'

There was a divide between professional soldiers and those who had been drafted into the war. Over 3 million Americans were involved in the Vietnam conflict and about two thirds of them were drafted. At the average age of 19 these were young men who were expected to do a 12-month 'tour of duty'. Many of these soldiers did not have a clear idea about why they were there. The experienced soldiers nicknamed the drafted ones 'cherries' because of their inexperience. Cherries were not popular:

- Experienced soldiers were expected to train them.
- Cherries made mistakes.
- Cherries replaced friends who had been killed or injured and were resented by the more experienced soldiers until they had proved themselves.

As a result:

- cherries were made to carry the heavy equipment like the 'field radio' and the M-60 machine gun
- cherries were put on 'point' – which meant guiding the platoon through the forest and checking for mines and booby traps. This meant they were more likely to be killed.

This situation created a great deal of stress and some historians believe it had a damaging effect on the Army's ability to fight.

Activity

1. Imagine you are a US soldier at the start of a 12-month tour of duty in Vietnam. Choose one or more of the following scenarios to write a diary entry about, describing your feelings and worries:
   - your first search and destroy mission – the experience of flying into enemy territory, landing at a 'hot LZ' (a landing zone under enemy fire), not being able to see the enemy, then helping your wounded friend back to the LZ for evacuation
   - the time you searched a South Vietnamese village for Viet Cong and your sergeant beat up an old woman to get information, and then burned down her house when she still did not say anything
   - what it is like to go on patrol and always be worried about mines and booby traps, and what the rest of your platoon felt like after three men were killed by mines
   - how you felt when you got letters from old friends back home that said Vietnam veterans were being spat on in the street by people who thought the war was wrong.

Follow up your enquiry

Research the story of Hamburger Hill (May, 1969). What impact do you think it had on soldiers when they felt there was no real point to what they were doing?

Source A: A stressed 1st Cavalry soldier is cheered by his buddy moments after an intense fire fight on a search and destroy mission 15 miles northwest of Tam Ky.

Activity

2. In groups discuss how experienced and inexperienced troops must have felt towards each other. Choose words or short sentences to list feelings. For each feeling listed, say what impact you think this would have on making each unit an effective fighting force.

As well as a division between professional and drafted soldiers, there was also racial tension between white and black troops. There was a widespread view that young black men were far more likely to be drafted than young white men.

'Fragging'

'Fragging' is the act of attacking a superior officer. In the past a 'fragmentation grenade' was used in such an attack, but in the Vietnam War it is believed that superior officers were usually shot. There are only 230 proven cases, but more than 730 others are suspected. A military force can only work if the troops obey their commanders. If troops were deliberately killing leaders who they thought were exposing them to unnecessary danger, then this suggests that the Vietnam War had a very significant impact on the US Army.

Drugs

The 1960s, rightly or wrongly, will go down in history as the 'swinging sixties'. It is seen as a decade of massive social and cultural change – particularly in Western Europe and the USA. These changes were to do with increased personal freedom, civil rights, the growth of popular music, increased sexual freedom, and experimentation with drugs. The Vietnam War was fought against this background.

While it is difficult to be certain about the extent of drug use by US soldiers during the war, it was a factor that affected the US Army's ability to fight. Marijuana, cocaine, LSD and amphetamines were believed to be used by US combat troops.

As US soldiers left Vietnam after their tour of duty they were given a medical examination. One senior Army commander reported, 'The Vietnam drug situation is extremely serious'.

The impact of the war on military discipline and morale increased as the conflict went on. After President Nixon started his policy of Vietnamisation (see page 42), US troops started to be withdrawn from Vietnam in large numbers. Because they knew they would soon be going home, soldiers still waiting to be withdrawn resented any orders that put them at increased risk. Morale suffered and it was harder to enforce military discipline.

Follow up your enquiry

Research the author and director of the film Platoon. Why was director Oliver Stone keen to show 'fragging' in his portrayal of the Vietnam War?

Source B: Nigel Cawthorne, *Vietnam: A War Lost and Won*, 2008.

In 1969 and 1970 alone, around 16,000 GIs received a dishonourable discharge [were sacked from the army] for possession... A report issued by the Pentagon in 1973 estimated that 35 per cent of all enlisted men in the Army who had served in Vietnam had tried heroin and 20 per cent had been addicted at some point during their tour [of duty]... Some restricted their [marijuana] smoking to off-duty hours, while others began smoking dope as soon as they woke. Men would run the risk of going out on patrol high, hallucinating, or paranoid on weed, or even tripping out on acid.

Source C: Statistics given by General William C. Westmoreland (commander of US forces in Vietnam, 1964–68), taken from the website of the Vietnam Helicopter Flight Crew Network (VHFCN). The VHFCN says it is a myth that most US soldiers were addicted to drugs, guilt-ridden about their role in the war, and deliberately used cruel and inhumane tactics.

- 91% of Vietnam veterans say they are glad they served.
- 74% said they would serve again even knowing the outcome.
- There is no difference in drug usage between Vietnam veterans and non-veterans of the same age group.

Activity

3. Discuss in groups why drug use would be a problem for an army in a war situation.

The impact of the war on US civilians

The Vietnam War had a major impact on people in the USA, and continues to cast a long shadow even today. The most obvious way in which the war had an impact on civilian life was the anti-war movement. You can read more about that on pages 36–43. However, people in the USA did not only react to the war by protesting against it. Some Americans thought the war was right but that it was being handled poorly. Some thought winning the war against communism was worth the cost in lives and money. Some thought that the war was right because the USA was always right. There were many different reasons why people supported the war and opposed the war, and for many people perhaps, the war was just something going on in the news that they did not pay a lot of attention to. You can find out more about these issues in Part B of this book.

Apart from those people who had family or friends involved in the war, most Americans were affected by the war through the media. Vietnam was very heavily reported: there were journalists and photographers with the troops and camera crews on assignment and covering major news stories. US civilians saw what was happening to US soldiers in great detail, in a way that had never happened before. They saw them wounded and killed, but perhaps even worse than that they saw US soldiers beating prisoners and intimidating civilians. Americans had never thought of their soldiers acting this way in other wars, and some of them thought Vietnam had had a terrible effect on these soldiers.

Source D: A US soldier in Saigon, 1969, photographed by famous war photographer Tim Page. Helmets were often used to say something about soldiers' feelings and identity. Why do you think this soldier has written 'hippie' on his?

Source E: Cover of *Life* magazine, February 1966: Wounded GIs

This muddy trench looks like something from the First World War.

The caption together with the picture suggests that the war is not going on in a good way – readers should be concerned.

This soldier's eyes have been damaged; he looks helpless.

His hand is reaching out as if trying to work out if anyone is there.

This soldier looks exhausted and cold.

He seems to be holding his mug and his comrade for comfort.

Source F: Cover of *Life* magazine, November 1965: A Viet Cong prisoner awaits interrogation

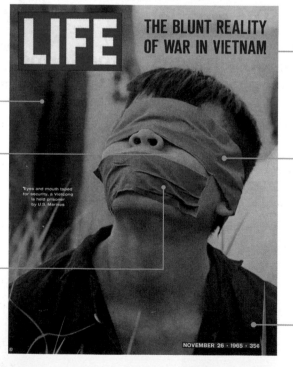

The figure in the background is a US soldier. He seems a menacing, powerful figure. His hand looks as though it is bunching into a fist.

The caption suggests that this sort of treatment of captives is a hard fact of the war in Vietnam.

The captive has been blindfolded to disorientate him.

The man seems to be straining to hear or perhaps to breathe. He looks helpless and afraid.

The captive has been gagged to make him powerless.

This man is not dressed as a soldier. Is he a civilian or Viet Cong?

Activity

4. Sources E and F are both covers from the popular US magazine, *Life*. What impact do you think each of these images would have had on US civilians?

Follow up your enquiry

Many films have been made about Vietnam by US filmmakers. These can be an interesting area for enquiry, although some of the films carry an 18 certificate so you will only be able to read about those. The following represent a range of approaches:

- *The Green Berets*, 1968 (certificate PG) is an anti-communist, pro-war take on Vietnam, featuring John Wayne, who decided to make the film because he was disgusted by the anti-war movement in the US.
- *The Deer Hunter* (1978) (certificate 18) follows three American friends, working men who go to Vietnam, and looks at the impact of war on them and their families.
- *Platoon* (1987) (certificate 15) looks at how the war brutalised US soldiers.
- *Forrest Gump* (1994) (certificate 12) tells the story of the USA in the 1960s to the 1980s through the life of Forrest Gump, including his experiences in Vietnam.

Veterans of the Vietnam War have often reported that when they went home no one who had not been in Vietnam could understand what they had been through. It was a common experience for veterans also to feel that people in the USA were ashamed of the Vietnam War and did not want to talk about it. Soldiers in Vietnam knew this was happening at home and it had a big impact on morale.

The impact of the war on South Vietnamese and North Vietnamese civilians

For the people of Vietnam, US involvement was only one part in a long-running civil war that stretched from 1945 to 1975. Over such a long period of time, war had a huge impact.

Source G: Rudolph Rummel, *Statistics of Vietnamese Democide: Estimates, Calculations, and Sources*, 1997. Rummel has put together estimates from many different sources. The estimates are grouped into three types: low, medium and high. He explains in this article that accurate figures are very hard to find.

Deaths in the North Vietnam vs. South Vietnam, US and others conflict, 1960–75

Category	Year range	Low estimate	Medium estimate	High estimate
North Vietnamese civilian deaths from bombing	1965–1972	-	65,000	-
North Vietnamese soldiers killed	1965–1972	-	500,000	-
Viet Cong deaths	1960–1975	172,000	251,000	329,000
Viet Cong and North Vietnamese soldiers deaths combined	1960–1975	533,000	1,011,000	1,489,000
South Vietnamese civilian deaths from gunfire/bombing	1960–1975	361,000	391,000	720,000
South Vietnamese soldiers killed	1960–1975	219,000	266,000	313,000
US military deaths	1960–1973	46,000	47,000	58,000

Activities

5. What does Source G tell you about the impact of the war on Vietnamese civilians? Consider:
   - figures for North Vietnam compared with those for South Vietnam
   - figures for civilian losses compared with military losses
   - information given about the causes of the civilian deaths.

6. What are the strengths and weaknesses of this source? Think about:
   - how reliable the source is: can you trust it to be accurate?
   - what level of detail it provides: what is its focus?

Impact on South Vietnamese civilians

Instead of feeling that US and ARVN troops were protecting them, many South Vietnamese thought of them as the enemy. These troops very rarely respected Vietnamese people or customs and were often brutal. In the countryside, particularly, people did not see the Viet Cong as enemies but more like their brothers and sisters.

Source H: An extract from *Legacy of Discord: Voices of the Vietnam War Era*, by Gil Dorland. This is a book of interviews and here Gil Dorland interviews Le Ly Hayslip, who grew up as a peasant girl in a South Vietnamese village and joined the Viet Cong.

> In 1966 and '67, I went to many villagers to sell goods on the black market. I witnessed a lot of cruelty. Americans kicked and beat old village men. When some children asked GIs [US soldiers] not to walk in the rice paddies, they beat the children's heads. GIs beat fathers in front of their children. It was much easier to take a beating in a torture camp than to have their pride and inner feelings shamed. There was no way the villagers could express to the American GIs their feelings, their anger, their hurt. They couldn't even cry. How could these villagers watch their wives raped in front of them, their husbands tortured and their children killed or wounded? They had to deal with that day in and day out for many years. Some GIs were nice to the villagers and children, but most were racist. They hated us, not only because we were their enemy but also because we were different in color and size. Their insults and foul language were often directed at us as a race, not as an enemy.

Activity

7. What does Source H tell you about the impact of the war on Vietnamese civilians? Consider:
   - who the source is and how reliable this account might be
   - what level of detail it provides: is it a general description or quite a specific one?
   - whether you have other information you could use to confirm whether many civilians suffered this sort of abuse from US soldiers.

Impact on North Vietnamese civilians

Source G shows that 65,000 people are estimated to have been killed by US bombing of North Vietnam. The North Vietnamese leaders told their people they could beat the USA if only they stood firm. The people in North Vietnam may have had little choice but to obey their leaders, but it seems as though they truly wanted to protect their country. They felt under attack from the capitalist USA. After every bombing raid, it was reported that thousands of people would emerge from shelters and start to repair the damage.

Source I: From the North Vietnamese government publication *Haiphong, a Steel Fortress*.

> ... in South Vietnam the US aggressors have put into practice the so-called 'rolling thunder plan' by carrying out repeated ferocious attacks against many North Vietnamese localities, among which Haiphong has been one of their main objectives.
>
> [US aeroplanes] have wantonly bombed many populous quarters and economic establishments inside and outside the City. But they have met with a dense network of anti-aircraft fire of the army and people of Haiphong and have been duly punished.
>
> Over the past forty days Haiphong has grown in strength in the fight and won victorious victories. From April 26, 1967 to October 11, 1967 the army and people of Haiphong shot down 161 U.S. airplanes and killed or captured many US pilots.

Source J: Front cover of *Life* magazine, 7 April 1967

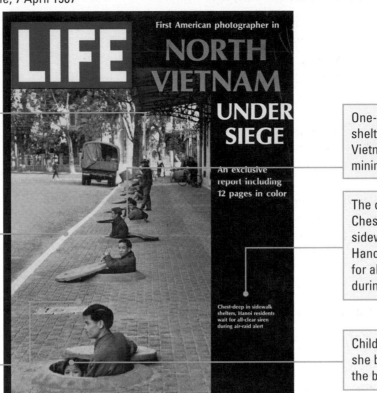

People seem eager to work. Reporters noted that civilians tried to continue to work despite the bombing.

This Hanoi street shows no sign of damage and is clean and pleasant. Was it chosen specially to show US readers that the bombing was failing?

The men do not look frightened but alert and watchful.

One-person bomb shelters: North Vietnam wanted to minimise casualties

The caption reads: Chest deep in sidewalk shelters, Hanoi residents wait for all-clear siren during air-raid alert.

Child sheltering: would she be frightened by the bombing?

Activities

8. Consider Sources I and J. What do they tell you about North Vietnamese people's reaction to US bombing? Some pointers have been added to Source J to help you with this.

9. Source I is written as government propaganda; Source J is from a US magazine but the photographer was only allowed to take pictures of scenes approved by the North Vietnamese government. How does government control like this affect what we know about how the war affected North Vietnamese civilians?

Case study: the My Lai massacre

The My Lai massacre combines several of the themes we have discussed in this section. One key question is whether My Lai was an exceptional incident, or whether other massacres like this were carried out by US troops in Vietnam.

On 16 March 1968, two platoons from Charlie Company were sent into the village of My Lai. Charlie Company had been taken by helicopter into the region because of incorrect reports that a battalion of Viet Cong were based in there. There were actually no Viet Cong soldiers in the village.

As the platoons entered the village, some villagers ran away. The US soldiers shot them. They then went through the village shooting and throwing grenades into the houses. The soldiers rounded up villagers. They raped village girls and then shot them. Survivors were forced into a ditch: all unarmed women, children and old men. The commander of the 1st Platoon, Lieutenant William L. Calley, ordered his men to shoot into the pile of people. They fired and fired. A two-year-old boy was still alive. He climbed out of the ditch, trying to escape, but Calley threw him back on the pile of corpses and shot him.

The company commander reported that 90 enemy soldiers had been killed, with no civilian casualties. His boss, improving the figures even more, reported that 128 enemy had been killed. It is not possible to be sure of the actual figures, but it is thought that at least 347 civilians were actually killed. Some of the bodies were mutilated after death.

The troops involved in the My Lai massacre did not think they had done anything wrong, and boasted about it. The Viet Cong publicised the massacre as a US atrocity. The US army covered up the incident, but reports of it gradually filtered through and finally it was reported by the media. US civilians were appalled and public reaction around the world condemned the massacre. Politicians demanded an inquiry into what had gone wrong and a trial of those involved.

Charlie Company and the Viet Cong

Before the My Lai massacre, Charlie Company had suffered badly from Viet Cong attacks. In February 1968, four men were hit by sniper fire and two men were killed by booby traps in one mission. On their next mission they walked into a minefield: 32 men were killed or wounded. In March, four men were killed by a booby trap. In the month before the My Lai massacre, the company (around 100 men) had lost 40% of its men to the Viet Cong – and they had never once seen the enemy.

Lieutenant Calley

Calley was charged with murder in September 1969. The US military portrayed the My Lai massacre as his fault. In the end, he was the only person convicted for the crimes at My Lai. He was sentenced to life imprisonment, but released after three and a half years.

However, many US observers of the trial supported Calley very strongly. In polls of the US public, 80% who responded thought he should not be convicted. There were several reasons for this:

- Some thought he was right to kill the Vietnamese civilians at My Lai because they were probably supporting the Viet Cong.
- Some blamed the US Army for putting a young, inexperienced, poorly educated man in command of a platoon.
- Many thought the case showed that the Vietnam War was brutalising and corrupting American boys.
- Calley said, 'Personally, I didn't kill any Vietnamese that day. I mean personally. I represented the United States of America.'

US attitudes to South Vietnamese civilians

US troops in Vietnam knew that they could not trust South Vietnamese people, because so many of them helped the Viet Cong. All troops had heard about women and children laying mines and throwing grenades. Children might be innocent now, but they would soon grow up to be Viet Cong, so why take the risk? Many US soldiers did not see Vietnamese civilians as human beings.

Search and destroy

These missions were disorientating. Troops were often flown in by helicopter, sometimes under fire. When they arrived, they did not know what they might be facing. The mission would be based on intelligence reports, but these were often faulty. Company and platoon leaders on the ground were given a lot of responsibility for coming to their own conclusions about what they should do and how they should act.

Source K: Scene from the My Lai massacre: the victims are women and young children.

Activities

10. Discuss with others why you think the My Lai massacre happened. You could make a chart like this one to record key points. The third column is to record anything that still does not make sense to you – there may be lots of points to write here. The first rows have been started for you.

Key issue	The effect at My Lai	But why?
Effects of fighting the Viet Cong	Was Charlie Company looking for revenge at My Lai?	Why did Charlie Company kill helpless children?
Inexperience of leadership	Calley was poorly prepared for his role	Surely Calley knew not to kill innocent people?
Troops' view of South Vietnamese civilians	Troops thought the villagers were Viet Cong supporters	Why did they think this?
Nature of search and destroy missions		

11. Do you think what happened at My Lai was typical of the way US soldiers behaved in Vietnam, or an exceptional case? It may be useful to look at your unanswered 'But why?' questions from the previous activity.

12. Write a report on My Lai as though you were a South Vietnamese journalist. What would say to your South Vietnamese readers about what had happened? What demands would you make of the US government to make sure it never happened again?

13. What, if anything, do you think the US leaders could have done differently to 'win hearts and minds' in Vietnam and among the US public?

 Your conclusion so far

From this topic, we have seen:

- The Vietnam War had a disastrous impact on those fighting it and on civilians. Hundreds of thousands of soldiers died; hundreds of thousands of civilians died.
- The US military was badly affected by the war. There were serious problems with morale and discipline, and with leadership and strategy.
- US civilians also suffered because of the war: apart from those who lost friends and relatives, all US citizens experienced losing a war that was hard to justify.
- Vietnamese civilians suffered most of all, perhaps: especially in the South where they were killed by both sides, in a war that was supposed to be about protecting them from harm.

From what you have learned in this topic, what do you think the impact of the Vietnam War was on civilians and the military? To answer this question:

- describe the impact of the war on the US military and US civilians
- describe the impact of the war on South Vietnamese and North Vietnamese civilians
- explain how impacts connected to create a downward spiral for US troops
- explain how impacts connected to create an upward spiral for the North Vietnamese.

A4 The growth of protest in the USA and the end of the conflict

Learning outcomes

By the end of this topic, you should be able to:

- identify some of the factors that led to protest in the USA
- describe the growth of this protest
- discuss turning points in the growth of protest in the USA
- decide for yourself why the USA lost the war.

Why did some people oppose the war?

The US government's justifications for the Vietnam War did not connect with all Americans. There were many reasons why. For instance:

- Americans found it difficult to identify with the South Vietnamese.
- US forces did not appear to be winning the war.
- Many young Americans were dying for something that seemed to have no point at all.
- TV and photojournalism brought the horrors of the war right into US living rooms.
- US presidents did not always tell the truth about the way the war was going or what the USA was doing to try and win it.

What is protest?

While many people may have disagreed with the way the war was being run, not everyone did something about it. When we are looking at the growth of protest, we are looking at action. Broadly speaking, people protested against the war through:

- demonstrations
- burning draft cards – draft resistance

- doing something to avoid the draft, such as leaving the USA
- violence – against themselves, against property and against others, for example the police.

Activities

1. What do you object to? What could you do to show your opposition? Of these methods of protest, which are legal and which are not? Which would be most effective in getting attention for your cause?

2. Find out some of the ways in which young men avoided being drafted.

3. Demonstrations are designed to get the government's attention and convince others to support a cause. Draft avoiders did not want to go to Vietnam. Are these both types of protest? Explain your answer.

Why did people protest?

As your research will show you, it was not one single reason that made some people in the USA decide the war was wrong and that they had to do something about it. Reasons changed over time as well. There were some important turning points in the growth of protest. Also, it is important to remember that the majority of Americans continued to support the way the war was being run (see page 59 in Part B). Some thought they should support their country whatever it did.

However, there are some basic building blocks of the protest. You might add some more to this list, but let's start with:

- the anti-war movement
- the influence of veterans
- opposition to the draft
- links to the civil rights movement
- the influence of the media.

The anti-war movement believed:

- the war was morally wrong
- the USA was lying to its people
- the war was corrupting young US soldiers through drugs and mindless violence
- the South Vietnamese government was corrupt; the North Vietnamese were fighting for freedom.

Influence of veterans:

- Some veterans of the fighting joined the protests.
- Their stories of brutality and pointless suffering were very powerful.
- Some veterans gave back medals they had won to show their opposition.
- It was hard for supporters of the war to dismiss veterans' opposition.

WHY DID PEOPLE PROTEST?

Opposition to the draft:

- The draft was unfair – many middle-class white Americans managed to avoid it; working-class and black Americans got drafted.
- In 1970 the system was changed to a fairer lottery – but many still tried to avoid it.

Links to the civil rights movement:

- Black Americans often felt they were being sent to Vietnam while white Americans avoided the draft.
- There was already a protest movement around civil rights which influenced the protests about Vietnam.

Influence of the media:

- The Vietnam War was called the 'first televised war'.
- Horrific scenes brought the war home to the USA.
- TV and photojournalism coverage weakened government attempts to justify the war.

Activities

4. Imagine you are a young American in 1970. Describe how you feel about the war in Vietnam.
5. Think about the recent war in Iraq or the war in Afghanistan. What factors influence how you feel about those conflicts? Ask a range of people for their opinions about these wars and why they feel that way.

The growth of protest

At the start of the Vietnam War, very few Americans were against it, but as the war went on, opposition increased. As we have seen, people thought the war was wrong for many different reasons. Not everyone who opposed the war also protested against it, but many hundreds of thousands did.

Anti-war demonstrations

There were lots of very big public demonstrations against the war, and the numbers of demonstrations and the numbers of people involved in them grew and developed as the war went on. Source A shows some information on demonstrations. You could add to this from your own enquiry.

Source A: Demonstrations against the war.

December 1964	25,000 people marched against the war in Washington DC
October 1965	100,000 people demonstrated in many cities across the USA
November 1965	25,000 people demonstrated in Washington DC (at the White House)
March 1966	20,000 people demonstrated in New York City
April 1967	400,000 people demonstrated in New York City
October 1967	100,000 demonstrated in Washington DC
August 1968	There were major demonstrations in Chicago
October 1969	2 million people took part in Vietnam Moratorium protests across the USA
November 1969	500,000 people demonstrated in Washington DC and 500,000 in San Francisco
May 1970	100,000 demonstrators protested in Washington DC
April 1971	500,000 people marched in Washington DC

Follow up your enquiry

Find out more about a major anti-war demonstration. See if you can discover:

- who organised it
- how it was reported – was it criticised or supported by the media?
- what its aims were.

Protesting against the draft

In July 1965 President Johnson increased the numbers of men to be conscripted – drafted – to fight in Vietnam. This increased protest against the war and produced a specific form of protest: burning of draft cards. It was illegal to burn your draft card and so when people burned their cards in public it was a strong form of protest. As well as burning cards, anti-war protestors also organised national draft card turn-ins – a thousand cards were returned in 1967.

In 1967, the world-famous boxer Muhammad Ali was drafted. He refused to go to Vietnam, saying: 'I ain't got no quarrel with those Viet Cong, anyway. They never called me nigger.' He was stripped of his titles, fined $10,000 and sentenced to five years in prison. This made him a hero to other anti-war protestors.

Source B: This photo shows Muhammad Ali (on the left) with Martin Luther King (on the right), answering questions about his decision to refuse the draft. Martin Luther King also protested against the war.

Activity

6. To what extent do you think famous black Americans like Muhammad Ali or Martin Luther King influenced the growth of protest? Consider:
   - media publicity
   - whether they were inspirational to those who respected them
   - mixed messages – would their involvement make white people think this was a black civil rights issue?
   - whether it would encourage opponents of black civil rights protests to oppose the anti-war movement too
   - whether individuals ever do more than just provide publicity for what is already happening.

Protests by Vietnam veterans

The protests by Vietnam veterans were a very significant part of the anti-war movement. It was hard for critics of the protests to dismiss these veterans as hippies or cowards: they had fought for their country and returned to explain why the war was wrong. One organisation of anti-war veterans is Vietnam Veterans Against the War (VVAW):

- In April 1967 six veterans marched together against the war in a demonstration in New York City (see Source A). They started VVAW.
- By 1969 VVAW had several hundred members.
- In 1970 membership grew from 1,500 to around 5,000 veterans.
- In 1971 membership peaked at around 30,000.

As well as marching in demonstrations, anti-war Vietnam veterans protested by returning medals to the government. These events had huge media impact and showed how completely some veterans rejected the war and all it stood for.

Activities

7. Why was media attention important for protest movements like VVAW?
8. During the course of the war, over 500,000 men deserted the US Army. Was this also a protest?

Other types of protest

Your research will show you that protests grew and developed in many different ways, for example there were increasing numbers of student sit-ins where students and teaching staff would sit together and refuse to be moved. There were acts of protest from within government – leaks of information, for example. There were violent protests and even cases where people set themselves on fire as a protest against the war. Popular culture – for example music, films, fashion, magazines – was also an important part of the growth of protest. Anti-war songs, and songs with negative references to US involvement in Vietnam, were very popular.

Activity

9. In what ways would songs that criticised the war have helped the growth of anti-war protests?

Source C: A photo of John Lennon and Yoko Ono in 1969. They strongly supported the anti-war movement.

Follow up your enquiry

Working in groups, find out about the anti-Vietnam War protest song 'Eve of Destruction', which was performed by Barry McGuire.

What messages does it give about the war?

How many copies did it sell and what might this mean about its influence on people in the USA?

Make a short PowerPoint presentation about the song and your findings.

Explaining the growth of protest

Protest against the Vietnam War changed over time. In some years there was more protest and in some years less. Some changes were in response to particular events. Some of the protest was linked to bigger, underlying changes in US society. Sometimes protest was organised and sometimes it was more spontaneous and individual. Explaining the growth of protest against the war is about making links and thinking about the ways in which these factors worked together.

The different types of protest are like different kinds of plants. The seeds are all in the soil, but they need the right kind of conditions to grow.

ResultsPlus
Top Tip

Remember to back up your points with precisely selected information for top marks. You could use information from page 41 to show that the Tet Offensive boosted protest against the war.

Sunlight is like the war: there would be no protest without it. The brighter the light, the more the 'protest plants' grow.

Some types of protest might grow faster and more strongly than others because they suit the conditions the best.

The soil could be US society. The big social changes affecting young people, civil rights, popular culture, women, changes in the media – all gave protest very fertile conditions to grow in.

Sometimes particular events gave protest against the war a massive boost; sometimes this might boost one type of protest in particular, like watering just one seedling and not the rest. These events are called turning points.

Fertiliser on the soil helps the plants to grow more quickly and strongly. When the media gives protest lots of dramatic coverage it has the same sort of effect.

The pot could represent organisations. Some organisations gave protests the right structure to help them grow; other organisations were the wrong shape and size.

Organisations

Big protests need lots of organising: publicity so people turn up, promotion so people want to take part, liaison with authorities so the protest can take place, and invitations to guest speakers or important public figures.

One important organisation in the anti-war movement was Students for a Democratic Society (SDS), a radical student organisation dedicated to reforming US society. It only became popular when growing numbers of students started to oppose the Vietnam War. The SDS recognised that no one was coordinating this opposition, so they took it on.

At first there were only a few SDS groups at a few universities, organising local demonstrations and sit-ins. Then the media started to publicise them. More and more SDS groups were set up. The SDS and other organisations put together big demonstrations and led the marchers. In 1968 the SDS organised a student strike involving more than a million students. By 1969 divisions in the SDS saw a radical wing split off: the Weathermen. They became involved in violence against the state.

Activities

10. Do you think organisations like the SDS caused the growth of protest or 'rode on the back of it'?

11. Look back at pages 30 (*Life* Magazine) and 33–35 (the My Lai massacre). Give examples to show how media coverage of the war encouraged protest.

Big social changes

Youth culture in the 1960s went in a different direction from the conventional US way of life. Some young people who rejected the rules of their parents' generation 'dropped out'. There were tensions between groups in society: on one hand there were those who believed that the USA must change to be truly free and fair for all, on the other hand those who felt traditional US values had to be defended.

There was also a gradual shift in the way many Americans thought about their leadership. In the 1950s most Americans trusted their leaders to do the right thing. By the 1970s, many people had lost that trust. The media had exposed how leaders had lied, covered things up, cheated and stolen, and so to a large extent Americans no longer believed what politicians told them. That made it harder for the US leaders to combat the growth of protest with their own message about why the war was justified.

Turning points

Many Americans changed their views about the Vietnam War in response to particular events. If events made a lot of people decide to protest or stop protesting, then we could call these turning points in the growth of protest.

One turning point in the growth of protest against the war was the Tet Offensive in January 1968, which you read about on pages 20–24. The Viet Cong had attacked deep into the heart of South Vietnam. The hugely influential TV journalist Walter Cronkite said, 'What the hell's going on here, I thought we were winning this war?' That was exactly what millions of Americans had been thinking, too.

During the offensive, 20 million TV viewers watched footage of General Nguyen Ngoc Loan, the South Vietnamese chief of police, executing a Viet Cong prisoner in cold blood. American viewers were horrified and many asked how the USA could be on the same side as those who executed prisoners in the street.

Source D: General Nguyen Ngoc Loan, the South Vietnamese chief of police, executes a Viet Cong prisoner during the Tet Offensive, South Vietnam, 1968. This photo is one of the iconic images of the Vietnam War. Why do you think this is?

Activities

12. What links can you make between social changes and the growth of anti-war protest?
13. How were organisations like the SDS linked to these social changes too?
14. Why do you think these big changes were going on in US society in the 1960s and 1970s?

Follow up your enquiry

Make sure you research other turning points in public opinion about the war, such as the My Lai massacre and the Kent State shootings (see pages 33–35 and 62–65). You should be able to explain how they affected the growth of protest in the USA.

Activities

15. List ways in which different factors in the anti-war movement came together with the Tet Offensive. Use the plant picture to help you.
16. List your top ten reasons for the growth of protest in the USA, showing why each one was important.

Looking for a way out

US fighting ended on 27 January 1973 when the USA, North Vietnam, South Vietnam and the Viet Cong signed 'An Agreement Ending the War and Restoring the Peace in Vietnam'. President Nixon said that this agreement meant 'We have finally achieved peace with honor.' But was this peace with honour, and how had it been achieved?

Nixon became president in 1969 with the promise of a 'secret plan' to end the war. It is not entirely clear what this secret plan was, but he started off with a two-pronged approach:

1. Vietnamisation – South Vietnamese forces were strengthened so they could defend themselves better, allowing US forces to go home. Opposition to the war dropped immediately. Vietnamisation started in 1969 and by the end of that year 60,000 US troops had been withdrawn.

2. There was a massive increase in bombing, trying to convince the North to admit defeat. North Vietnamese troops also had sanctuaries in Cambodia so that was bombed too. This had to be done in secret because Cambodia was a neutral country. Nixon was taking a huge risk with US and international opinion – no one wanted to see the war spread any further.

Activity

17. What do you think of Nixon's strategy to end the war? What are its strong points and are there any weak points that you can see?

Bringing US troops home was very popular in America and really reduced opposition to the war for a while, but there were problems with Vietnamisation. The South Vietnamese troops were very well equipped and trained by the USA, and sometimes fought well, but they could not seem to beat the North Vietnamese. And the increased bombing did not seem to have any real impact on North Vietnamese morale.

The invasion of Cambodia

Frustrated, Nixon decided to launch a ground invasion of Cambodia to destroy the sanctuaries. He used ARVN troops, with US air support. The invasion of Cambodia appalled many Americans: Nixon was supposed to be ending the war, not escalating it. The US Congress began to reduce its support for the war and so the president had to step back from trying to win the war by military means.

Diplomacy – a final gamble?

Nixon pushed for a diplomatic solution. At first he and his negotiating team hoped to convince North Vietnam to agree to terms that would protect South Vietnam but this was not easy to achieve. Diplomacy is a bit like a game of cards, and North Vietnam still had a strong hand to play.

USA

North Vietnam

Activities

18. Weigh up the evidence: who do you think had the strongest hand in the negotiations?

19. In groups, act out a diplomatic meeting between the USA and North Vietnam.

    • The first thing to do is decide as a diplomatic team what you want to achieve. What is the best result you could hope for and what is thc minimum you could live with? (See the Fact file for a summary of what was actually agreed.)

    • You can back up your discussions with the arguments listed on the playing cards, plus any other factors you have researched.

    • Keep your best arguments and threats in reserve; try to reach some agreements on minor points first to get things moving.

Fact file: the Paris Peace Accords, 1973

1. A ceasefire to be agreed between North and South Vietnam.

2. The USA to start withdrawing troops as soon as the ceasefire is in place: to be complete in 60 days.

3. US prisoners of war to be returned.

4. Some sort of a political solution to the situation in the South would follow: free elections, etc.

5. Peaceful reunification of Vietnam to be achieved.

The end of the conflict and what happened next

The agreement, signed in Paris in January 1973, which Nixon claimed was 'peace with honor', was a smokescreen. North Vietnam was never going to agree to an independent South Vietnam. Even when they were being bombed by the USA and pressurised by the USSR and China, North Vietnam would not budge.

The best the USA could get was agreement that there would be a ceasefire first and then a political solution 'later', plus an exchange of prisoners of war. This allowed the USA to leave Vietnam with the conflict halted. But despite US promises to support South Vietnam, Congress blocked any more military spending and when, after two years of skirmishes, North Vietnam launched an offensive in December 1974, resistance in the South collapsed and South Vietnam surrendered on 30 April 1975.

Despite fears that the North would unleash a bloodbath on the South, this didn't happen. Thousands of people were sent for 're-education' but the real suffering came when the USA led the rest of the non-communist world in shunning the new nation and causing its economy to collapse. Hundreds of thousands fled the country.

Your conclusion so far

From this topic, we have seen:

• There were many reasons why some people protested against the Vietnam War.

• Protest grew and developed as the war continued.

• Nixon promised to end the war 'with honour' but North Vietnam had everything to gain from not giving in.

• Nixon abandoned South Vietnam under a smokescreen agreement.

From what you have learned in this topic, why do you think the USA lost the Vietnam War?

To answer this question:

• identify the strengths and weaknesses of both sides

• explain North Vietnam's advantages over the USA's weak position

• consider the importance of public opinion as a factor on both sides

• consider whether the USA had an achievable objective in Vietnam. Was there a way it could have 'won'?

Enquiry and writing skills support

Learning outcomes

By the end of this section, you should be able to:

• follow up an enquiry
• select and organise your material
• write up your enquiry.

In this section we will see how to complete the stages of following up an enquiry. The diagram on this page shows you the enquiry stages and what you need to do.

Controlled Assessment

Present your conclusions

Review and organise material – reach conclusions

Keep to the point of the enquiry

Don't get sidetracked

Identify key issues and follow up leads

Check what is useful

Check for reliability

Keep what is relevant to the enquiry

Relevant

STOP

Sift and sort material

Discard material irrelevant to enquiry

Irrelevant

What range of sources might be useful?
• Newspapers
• Letters and diaries
• Films and TV documentaries
• Oral accounts
• Paintings and photographs
• Others?

Identify and find sources

LIBRARY

Where can I find sources?
• School library
• Internet
• Textbooks
• Local library
• Others?

What is the enquiry about?

Following up an enquiry 1: The reasons for increasing US involvement in Vietnam from 1954 to 1964

Your controlled assessment Part A task will be similar to this one:

> **Enquiry focus**
>
> Your enquiry task will focus on the reasons for increasing US involvement in Vietnam from 1954 to 1964.

In this practice example, we are going to follow up this enquiry focus. You will be able to use the skills you develop to follow up your own Part A enquiry.

What is the enquiry about?

Your first step is to identify the precise enquiry. In this instance, it is about identifying factors that caused US involvement in Vietnam to increase over the specific time period.

This enquiry is trying to find out:

- why US involvement in Vietnam increased over the period 1954 to 1964
- which reasons were most important and why.

Identify and find sources

The next stage is to gather your information. Start with an easy outline book and read through the relevant material. Write some summary notes, making sure you include the book title, author and the pages where you have found the information. You should only start to look for more detailed information when you have used two or three textbooks which give you the basic information.

Begin by rereading pages 4–13 of this book and completing the activities below.

ResultsPlus

Top Tip

Good answers to Part A questions will include well-chosen short quotations from the books they use.

Activities

Making notes

1. Make a bullet point list of useful information from your first source of information. For example:
   - Kennedy worried that Diem was losing control and that South Vietnam would be taken over by the communists.
   - Johnson used the Gulf of Tonkin incident to justify increased US involvement in Vietnam.

2. Code the points on your list, or sort them into a chart like the one below.

President Kennedy's reasons for increased involvement	President Johnson's reasons for increased involvement

Part A: Carry out a historical enquiry

To add to your sources, you might start by doing a quick search on the internet but you should also look at books by historians. When you find a book, check the contents page and the index to make sure it covers the topic you want to research. You could also use TV documentaries as a source of information but be careful to check them against other sources to be sure they have not been dramatised or exaggerated.

ResultsPlus
Top Tip

Looking for information can be a slow process. You often read through a lot to get just a small piece of new information. Your work will be better though if you concentrate on what's new and relevant, rather than adding information that you already have or information that is not relevant.

Sift and sort material

Go through your new sources and make additional notes. It will help if you use a fresh page for each book or other source of information. Remember your enquiry is about reasons for increased US involvement in Vietnam. The book or the webpage you have found was not written to answer your specific enquiry. You have to choose what to take from your source to answer that – see activities 3 and 4 on page 47.

You will start to see the same sorts of ideas coming up in your sources. Treat these as leads for your enquiry. For example, you have already noted that the Gulf of Tonkin incident in 1964 was a reason for a massive increase in US involvement in Vietnam. Source A says that the Gulf of Tonkin incident gave President Johnson 'the excuse he wanted to take direct military action'. This suggests that:

- Johnson had already decided he wanted to escalate the war
- the Gulf of Tonkin incident was used to get the backing of Congress for escalation.

You could follow up these two leads, going through the same process of finding, sifting and sorting, and noting information.

Stick to the enquiry path

Don't go off track! Remember to keep to your enquiry path – and not to add in material which is not relevant. For example, the details of the types of ships that were involved in the Gulf of Tonkin incident may be interesting but these details do not help your enquiry about reasons for the USA's increased involvement in Vietnam.

Source A: An extract from *Modern World History Student Book* by Brodkin et al, 2009.

Increasing US involvement in Vietnam

Between 1954 and 1960, the USA sent equipment and military 'advisers' into South Vietnam. Meanwhile, the Viet Cong and North Vietnam were being supplied by China and the Soviet Union. From 1961 President Kennedy began increasing the number of advisers in South Vietnam until there were more than 11,000 US advisers in the country...

After Kennedy's assassination in 1963, President Johnson decided to increase American involvement in Vietnam. When North Vietnamese torpedo boats attacked American torpedo boats in the Gulf of Tonkin in 1964, it gave Johnson the excuse he wanted to take direct military action. As a result of the 'Tonkin incident' (in which no serious damage was done), Congress gave Johnson the authority to 'take all necessary steps, including the use of force' to defend South Vietnam.

Johnson's first move was to launch 'Operation Rolling Thunder' against North Vietnam, to stop it supplying the Viet Cong. The USA bombed factories, supply lines, ports and military bases. The idea was for the bombing to be so heavy that troops would not be needed. However, the bombing was unsuccessful, so in July 1965 180,000 American troops were sent to Vietnam.

Activities

Selecting information

3. Read Source A and decide with a partner how much of it is useful for the enquiry. Remember:

- you want to find out reasons why the US involvement in Vietnam increased from 1954 to 1964
- usually you only want new points
- you may want to make a note if two sources agree about an important point.

4. Photocopy or write out the whole passage. Colour-code it: green for new information about reasons, yellow for evidence of increased involvement and blue for duplicated information – information that repeats or agrees with what you have already got from other sources. Some parts have been done for you.

Use sources carefully

Sometimes you will also need to think about reliability. Be particularly careful about internet sources because they are sometimes anonymous and it is difficult to check the information they contain. They often express a particular political viewpoint, and you need to think about their purpose and possible bias. As you use your sources, apply the RDR tests – relevance, duplication and reliability.

Activity

Relevance and reliability

5. Study Source B. Decide with a partner which of the following statements you agree with. Then add any useful information to your notes.

The source:

- is not biased
- is biased but has useful information
- makes statements about the Gulf of Tonkin incident being a US fraud
- says the Gulf of Tonkin incident was due to honest mistakes by US forces
- suggests the USA may have provoked the second attack
- argues that Johnson deliberately used the incident to launch open attacks on North Vietnam
- suggests that the US government always intended to go to war in Vietnam
- argues that the USA never thought it would need a ground war against the Viet Cong
- is mainly relevant to this enquiry
- does not add much to this enquiry.

Source B: From *Workers World*. To celebrate its 50th year of publication the paper reprinted stories from the past. This is how it described the Gulf of Tonkin incident in its edition of 21 February 2008.

On Aug. 2 and 4, 1964, the Pentagon claimed that small Vietnamese boats had fired on the USS Maddox and another destroyer in the Gulf of Tonkin, off the coast of Vietnam. Lyndon Johnson used this alleged attack as pretext [excuse] for ramming [forcing] a resolution through Congress giving him the power and funds to wage war on Vietnam. Johnson's own papers later revealed it was a fraud, and then Defense Secretary Robert McNamara admitted in the film 'Fog of War' that the whole incident had been phony. Only two of the 100 senators voted against the resolution... The other 98 went along with the ruling-class war drive, as did the entire corporate media. Workers World Party's youth organization, Youth Against War and Fascism (YAWF), immediately challenged the Tonkin fraud and the war from the beginning.

Identify issues and follow up leads

Activities

6. Study Source C. It shows how the US Congress viewed the Tonkin incident, based on the information it had been given. What leads does this give you about why US involvement increased?

7. Add information from Source C to your notes. In your real enquiry, it will help if you add website details or textbook page numbers, in case you want to find the passage again.

8. Begin to organise your information under key headings whenever you use a new source.

   This enquiry has provided several new leads. In your real enquiry, you could use your leads as headings for your key issues.

   • President Johnson was keener to increase US involvement than Kennedy

   • both Kennedy and Johnson were motivated by the domino theory

   • the Gulf of Tonkin incident provided a justification for escalating the conflict

   • historians disagree about some of the reasons for increasing US involvement, for example was it deliberate or did the USA stumble into it?

Source C: An extract from the Tonkin Gulf Resolution, 1964.

... Naval units of the Communist regime in Vietnam... have deliberately and repeatedly attacked United States naval vessels [ships] lawfully present in international waters, and have thereby created a serious threat to international peace...

Follow up more leads

At this stage of your actual enquiry you would have a number of leads. For this example, follow up the leads identified, using the source file and other useful sources you have found. Review your material – can you identify any gaps which you need to research? What are the key areas that you should go into in more depth?

Source file

Source D: This extract from the 'Gulf of Tonkin' entry on the Spartacus Educational website describes the situation in the run-up to the 1964 presidential election.

Barry Goldwater, the right-wing Republican candidate for the presidency, called for an escalation of the war against the North Vietnamese. Johnson, on the other hand, argued that he was not willing: 'to send American boys nine or ten thousand miles away from home to do what Asian boys ought to be doing for themselves.'

In the election of November, 1964, the voters decided to reject Goldwater's aggressive policies against communism and Johnson won a landslide victory. What the American public did not know was that President Johnson was waiting until the election was over before carrying out the policies that had been advocated by his Republican opponent, Barry Goldwater.

Source E: From an interview with Roger Hilsman, in *Legacy of Discord: Voices of the Vietnam War Era*, by Gil Dorland, 2001. Hilsman was an adviser to Kennedy on Vietnam and was sacked by Johnson.

It became perfectly clear to me that Johnson wanted a war.... I think [Johnson's] motivation was some kind of simple-minded anticommunism. It was either black or white; whereas Kennedy recognized that the communists had different colors and shades. It wasn't just black and white.

Source F: An extract from *Ideology, Conflict and Retreat: The USA in Asia 1950–1973*, by Geoff Stewart.

The Tonkin Gulf Resolution was later used to cover the vast escalation of the war in 1965. Yet it is wrong to think that this was part of a well-planned strategy of deception. Johnson had no intention in 1964 of massively escalating the war or directly committing US troops. This arose from later circumstances. The resolution was merely designed to threaten North Vietnam and hearten the South. When, in 1968, the tide of opinion was turning against American intervention in Vietnam, which had become massive, details of the Gulf of Tonkin incident were picked over and portrayed as part of some sinister scheme [cooked up] by the president and his advisers.

Source G: Derrick Murphy, Kathryn Cooper and Mark Waldron, *United States 1776–1992*, 2001.

In the same year [1963] a plot to assassinate Diem was hatched by men within his own government [the government of South Vietnam: Diem was president]. The CIA knew the plan, as did the American ambassador in Saigon, but they saw him as a liability so did not stop it. Diem was murdered just a few weeks before Kennedy himself was assassinated in Dallas. General Westmoreland, the American military commander in Vietnam, said that this involvement in assassination made the USA morally obliged to stay in the country to sort out the mess.

Source H: An extract from President Eisenhower's news conference, 7 April 1954.

[Y]ou have broader considerations that might follow what you would call the 'falling domino' principle. You have a row of dominoes set up, you knock over the first one, and what will happen to the last one is the certainty that it will go over very quickly. So you could have a beginning of a disintegration that would have the most profound influences.

... Asia, after all, has already lost some 450 million of its peoples to the communist dictatorship, and we simply can't afford greater losses. But when we come to the possible sequence of events, the loss of Indochina, of Burma, of Thailand, of the Peninsula, and Indonesia following, now you begin to talk about... millions and millions and millions of people. ... So, the possible consequences of the loss are just incalculable to the free world.

Review and organise material – reach conclusions

Finally, you will need to reach a conclusion. You could summarise your key points in a concept map showing information about all the key issues.

Draw extra arrows to show how the factors link; for example, the failure of Diem to build a successful government in South Vietnam meant that the USA looked for ways to make North Vietnam back down, which led to plans to bomb North Vietnam, which led to the Gulf of Tonkin being used to justify an escalation of the war, which did not make North Vietnam back down, which meant the USA sent ground troops...

In this example enquiry, there are a lot of possible reasons to consider over the time period. The enquiry needs to show that you know what the main reasons are and can select relevant information from sources to support your answer. The conclusion is your opportunity to show you can also assess the information – to talk about how important each reason was. So in the case of this example enquiry it would make sense to use the conclusion to say which reason is the most important, in your view.

Present your conclusions

The following activities are practice for your controlled assessment task.

Activities

9. Make a set of notes to go with your concept map. Use the same headings. Do not use more than two sides of paper. You can include quotations from your sources in your notes.

10. Write up your enquiry. You can turn to 'Maximise your marks' on page 72 to get some tips on improving your answer.

Following up an enquiry 2: The extent of change in US military tactics after the Tet Offensive, 1968

This practice enquiry is different from enquiry 1. This second enquiry gives you practice in making comparisons and deciding to what extent tactics changed. This second enquiry would mean finding out what the main problems the USA faced in Vietnam over the period were and how they adapted tactics to deal with them. Follow the enquiry stages outlined on page 44. Identify, sift and sort your information.

Begin by using pages 16–24 of this book. Then go on to the information given in the source file. You can then follow up more leads if you like. Video footage of military tactics can be found on services like YouTube, for example search for clips from the *Battlefield Vietnam* series.

Remember to stick to the enquiry path when you follow up your leads, and remember the RDR tests (page 47). For example, many writers are extremely critical of US tactics, but this enquiry is about the extent to which tactics changed, not whether they were morally right or wrong.

Activities

11. Read pages 16–24 and the sources on pages 51–52. Make a bullet point list of useful information. For example:

    Before 1968

    - main tactics: bombing plus large-scale search and destroy missions
    - problems with bombing: it had almost no impact on the enemy's ability to fight
    - problems with search and destroy: it was dangerous for troops, alienated the local population and could lead to large-scale engagements that did not achieve much.

    After 1968

    - the Tet Offensive seriously reduced the Viet Cong's ability to fight
    - main US tactics: bombing plus small unit actions to gain control of the countryside
    - Vietnamisation was successful in enabling US troops to leave and to reduce casualties.

12. Begin to organise your notes. For this practice enquiry, you could arrange the tactics into a chart like the one page 51. Notes on tactics before 1968 have been started for you. Add details to each bullet point in the chart. You can also add new bullet points.

13. Now colour code your chart. Use green when military tactics were similar before and after 1968 and red for different methods.

14. How much change can you see?

ResultsPlus
Top Tip

Part A questions are often about change, for example about the nature of change, the factors involved in a change, or turning points that really show change in action.

Before 1968		
Political/military aims	Military problems	Military tactics
• To wear down enemy forces (attrition) • To stop movement of supplies and reinforcements down the Ho Chi Minh Trail • To deny the Viet Cong hiding places in South Vietnamese villages • To force North Vietnam to negotiate to end the war • To avoid antagonising China or the USSR into joining the conflict openly	• Enemy forces were highly resilient with a large supply of new recruits • Bombing/chemical warfare was largely ineffective but many planes were shot down • Search and destroy missions alienated the South Vietnamese population • It was hard to distinguish between enemy and allies • North Vietnam showed no sign of needing to negotiate – in fact was clearly winning the war • Military tactics did not seem to achieve anything meaningful to people back home in the USA • China and the USSR seemed to have little influence on North Vietnam	• Bombing and chemical weapons (Agent Orange, napalm) • Search and destroy, large unit sweeps • Overwhelming firepower, air support
After 1968		
Political/military aims	Military problems	Military tactics

Source file

Search-and-destroy missions did kill Viet Cong soldiers, but there were problems.

- The raids were often based on inadequate information.
- Inexperienced US troops often walked into traps.
- Innocent villages were mistaken for Viet Cong strongholds.
- Civilian casualties were extremely high in these raids. For every Viet Cong weapon captured by search-and-destroy, there was a body count of six. Many of these were innocent civilians.
- Search-and-destroy tactics made the US and South Vietnamese forces very unpopular with the peasants...

Despite the problems, in many ways US military tactics became more effective. The army shifted from large-unit sweeps of the search and destroy approach of 1966-67 to small-unit actions, which increased control of the countryside. By September 1969, 50 per cent of South Vietnam seemed under Saigon's control compared to only 20 per cent a year before. This was, of course, helped by the terrible hammering that the Viet Cong had taken in 1968.

Source C: An extract from *Vietnam, Korea and US Foreign Policy 1945-75,* by Christine Bragg.

The success of the Vietnamisation programme for the Nixon administration in the period 1969–71 is demonstrated by:

- the fall in the number of US casualties (see Figure 10.1)
- the withdrawal of military personnel (see Table 10.1).

Figure 10.1 Ratio of monthly US-KIA (killed in action) to troop levels during the Vietnam War

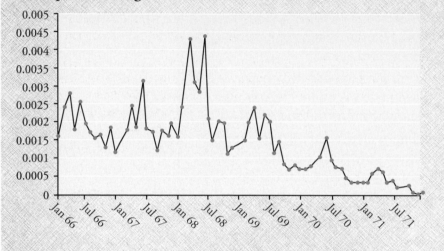

Table 10.1 US military strength in South Vietnam, 1969–72

Year	Troop Totals	Year	Troop Totals
Jan 1969	536,100	Jan 1971	334,600
June 1969	538,700	June 1971	239,200
Jan 1970	475,200	Jan 1972	156,800
June 1970	414,900	June 1972	47,000

Source D: From an interview with Roger Hilsman, advisor to President Kennedy, in *Legacy of Discord,* by Gil Dorland, 2001.

As an infantry commander in World War II, I had been bombed by the U.S. Air Force too many times to believe that bombing could win wars. Strategic bombing in my judgement doesn't work... The items of significance transported over the Ho Chi Minh Trail into South Vietnam were radio communication equipment and small-arms weapons. Hell, they were wheeling it down on bicycles. Bombing only showed the desperation of the United States to the Asians. Bombing has little effect in nonindustrial countries. What the hell was a bomb going to hit?

Writing up your answer

The moderator will be looking for four main things – that you have:

- kept your answer focused on the enquiry
- found information from different sources
- backed up your statements with information
- communicated your answer by organising it well and using good spelling, punctuation and grammar.

The activities which follow will help you to improve your writing. Remember to use the skills you have learned when you write up your controlled assessment answer.

Activities

Improving writing

15. Study example extracts 1 and 2, imagining you are the moderator. Discuss with a partner the good and bad points of each example. You will find the answers at the bottom of the page.

16. Suggest ways you could improve example extracts 1 and 2. You can do this in bullet point notes.

17. Study example extract 3. It is part of a high-level response. It compares methods, finding similarities and differences, and giving details. Now try adding to the answer by giving more examples to support the statements in each paragraph. You can also add more paragraphs giving similarities and differences.

Example extract 1

They were the same. On U Tube you can see bombing and it says bombing went on all through the war. It used bombs and also napalm which burned up everything it touched. But it didn't stop the Veit Kong.

Example extract 2

What happened in 1968 was the Tet Offensive. This was a significant turning point because the Viet Cong managed to attack 100 cities across South Vietnam, despite all the money and lives the US had spent on the war so far. People in the US couldn't believe it because they had been told the US was winning the war. Even though in fact the Tet Offensive was really a defeat for the Viet Cong. But it was hard for the US military to explain this defeat to people. It looked more like the US was being defeated in a foreign war: something that had never happened before. How was it that despite having the best army in the world and being a global superpower, the US couldn't beat a tiny Third World country?

One reason was that the US was not able to use as much force as it could have done because it was worried about China and the USSR joining in the war. Many US generals wanted to bomb North Vietnam 'back to the stone age', even to use nuclear weapons if all else failed. Hawks in US politics also supported invasions of Laos and Cambodia as well as of North Vietnam to cut the Viet Cong off from its safe areas and supplies. One difference after 1968 in tactics was that Nixon did permit small scale invasion of Cambodia, but the protests at home about this were enormous...

Example extract 3

Some military tactics continued after the Tet Offensive in 1968, like bombing for example. Bombing of targets in North Vietnam started in February 1965 and continued until 1972. It was massively expensive for the US and many pilots were lost. But the US believed that eventually North Vietnam would suffer so much damage that it would be forced to negotiate for peace. US politicians worried that if they did too much it would upset China, which had happened in the Korean War [sources quoted in the full answer]...

The Tet Offensive in 1968 did see the start of a change in tactics on the ground. Before Tet, General Westmoreland had developed large unit search and destroy tactics, based on locating Viet Cong forces and using helicopters to carry troops there to attack the enemy. But this was not always successful because information about the Viet Cong was unreliable, so the enemy might have disappeared or have set a trap. Search and destroy missions often meant South Vietnamese villages were destroyed and villagers killed: the very people the US was supposed to be protecting. And it was hard to explain military success to people in the US because US troops would fly in to an area, fight the enemy and then fly out again...

Tactics on the ground had to change. Small units now patrolled the countryside, building up good relations with the villages [answer gives examples, quoting sources]. But the biggest change was Vietnamisation. Huge amounts of money were spent supplying and training South Vietnamese forces, while US troops were withdrawn. By June 1972, only 42,000 troops were left, around 500,000 less than in 1969.

Summary

Success in your enquiry comes from:

- sticking to the focus of the enquiry
- using a range of sources, keeping their relevance and reliability in mind
- organising your answer to show good quality of written communication.

Example 1 does identify similarities, but it is not detailed enough and it does not identify any differences. It does not refer to any sources.

Example 2 has more detail and has made some comments about similarity and difference. But the student has got side-tracked. The answer is mainly about the reasons why the US military struggled in Vietnam. There is not enough about tactics. Example 2 does not refer to any sources.

Part B Representations of history

How did people in the US react to the Vietnam War?

Learning outcomes

By the end of this chapter, you should be able to:

- describe a range of reactions to the Vietnam War in the US
- understand the key issue of 'the vocal minority' and 'the silent majority'
- explain why historians disagree about reactions to the war.

In Part B of your controlled assessment you are exploring different ideas about the way people in the US reacted to the Vietnam War. Reactions varied a lot, and some people's reactions also changed as the war went on for years.

Historians are interested in these different reactions. They agree that the way people in the US reacted to the war had a major impact on the war and on America as a nation. But they disagree about what this impact was. For example:

- How much opposition was there?
- What were people opposing: the war or how it was handled?
- Did the protestors turn US opinion against the war, or were the protesters seen as unpatriotic by 'public opinion', which stayed in favour of the war for longer?

How do we know how people reacted to the Vietnam War?

The Vietnam War is often called 'the first televised war'. Every night on TV, people in the US saw the war for themselves, and they read about it every day in newspapers and magazines. Reactions were strong.

Compared to earlier conflicts, we have a lot of source material about what happened and what people thought about it: from tape recordings of presidents' private conversations to letters from mothers to their sons serving in the war.

So, do we know for sure how people in the US reacted to the Vietnam War? There are three main issues with this question.

☞ People reacted in lots of different ways and so the evidence points in lots of different directions.

? Most of the evidence about reactions relates to a relatively small number of people: we don't know much about what most people thought.

⚖ What politicians, journalists and campaigners said about the public's reactions was influenced by their own values and beliefs.

How do you think the evidence we have might be affected by people's personal beliefs?

Activities

1. What sort of things would turn public opinion against a war (e.g. deaths of soldiers)?
2. Why do you think democratic governments worried about public opinion?
3. What do democratic governments do to encourage public support for their wars?

Source A: Photo of an anti-Vietnam War demonstration in New York, 15 April, 1967.

Source B: A quote from Senator John Stennis about an anti-Vietnam War march in October 1967.

It is clear from the evidence that I have that this is a part of a move by the Communists, especially of North Vietnamese government, to divide the American people, disrupt our war effort, discredit our government before the entire world. The leaders of North Vietnam consider the March on the Pentagon tomorrow as much of their war effort as the guerrilla warfare in South Vietnam and the North Vietnamese army assaulting our troops on the battlefield. Those who participate in these demonstrations tomorrow will be, in effect, cooperating with and assisting our enemy.

Did you know?

You can watch the newsreel of the march from Source B on YouTube. Search for 'Vietnam War peace march, MLK leads procession'.

Activities

4. Study Source A. What does the photo show about the make-up of this crowd? Investigate these categories:
   - men and women
   - old and young
   - black and white
   - military personnel (look for uniforms).

5. Which words would you use to describe the impression this photograph gives you of the demonstration (for example: huge, peaceful)?

6. Do you think Source B is positive or negative about the demonstrators?

7. What about Source A: is it positive or negative? Can a photo express a view?

A range of reactions

In the USA, those who strongly supported America winning the war were known as 'hawks' and those who wanted to find a peaceful solution in Vietnam as quickly as possible were called 'doves'. So we can think about reactions to the war being divided into pro-war and anti-war reactions.

As you will also have seen in Part A, there were different reasons why people were for or against the war. So you also need to search the source for clues about which particular point of view it is coming from. Again, sometimes this is fairly easy, at other times you are going to need **context**.

> **Context:** the background information that helps you understand a source.

Activities

The badges in Source C are all from the Vietnam War era. People wore them to show what they thought about the war – and maybe for other reasons, like fashion, too.

8. Which badges are pro-war and which are anti-war? Write a list showing your choices.

9. What reactions to the war are shown by the badges? Use the following list to help you classify them. Match each badge against one of the items in the list (some badges can be used more than once).

Pro-war:
- the US should go all-out to win the war
- patriotic: support America!
- the war is right because it is against communism.

Anti-war:
- choose peace not war
- don't bomb North Vietnam
- messages linking the war to civil rights issues: equal treatment for women, black Americans, etc.
- messages telling people to do something specific.

Source C: Badges from the Vietnam War era.

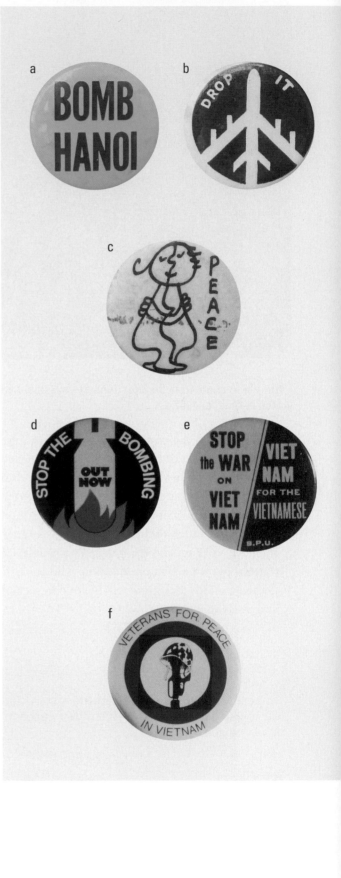

Decoding the message

Some of these badges rely on symbols to deliver their message. The peace symbol is a good example. The symbol originally came from the anti-nuclear weapons campaign, but over time it came to stand for 'peace, not war'. You can see the peace symbol combined with other symbols on some of the badges. For example, it is combined with the symbol for female (see badge k). When they are put together these two symbols mean 'women against the Vietnam War'. It is also combined with the characteristic silhouette of a B52 bomber (see badge b) to stand for an end to US bombing campaigns in Vietnam.

Activity

10. List the symbols used on the badges and your ideas about their meaning. Collaborate with the rest of your class to build up a complete list of symbols and ideas about meanings.

President Nixon believed the 'silent majority' supported his actions in continuing the war in Vietnam, unlike a tiny but noisy minority of protestors. Was that true, or was opposition much stronger and more significant? This is a key issue for you to explore, and we'll look at it in more detail on the next page.

A silent majority?

When Nixon became president he said he had a secret plan to end the war. By October 1969, with no sign of the war ending, around two million people took part in the 'Peace Moratorium': the largest demonstration in US history. On 3 November 1969, Nixon made a speech on TV about the war. He called for support from the 'great silent majority' of American people.

Source D: Address to the Nation on the War in Vietnam, 3 November, 1969. The pledge that Nixon refers to is his promise to bring peace.

> In San Francisco a few weeks ago, I saw demonstrators carrying signs reading: 'Lose in Vietnam, bring the boys home.' Well, one of the strengths of our free society is that any American has a right to reach that conclusion and to advocate that point of view. But as President of the United States, I would be untrue to my oath of office if I allowed the policy of this Nation to be dictated by the minority who hold that point of view and who try to impose it on the Nation by mounting demonstrations in the street…
>
> And so tonight – to you, the great silent majority of my fellow Americans – I ask for your support… The more support I can have from the American people, the sooner that pledge can be redeemed; for the more divided we are at home, the less likely the enemy is to negotiate… North Vietnam cannot defeat or humiliate the United States. Only Americans can do that.

A Gallup poll straight after the speech on 3 November 1969 showed that 77% of Americans supported Nixon's approach to the war. The White House received 50,000 telegrams and 30,000 letters that reinforced this support. Nixon quoted one letter in a speech, shown in Source E.

Source E: A letter read out by President Nixon in a speech to the US House of Representatives, 13 November 1969.

> Dear President Nixon:
> As a registered Democrat who did not vote for you in 1968, and a father with a son in Vietnam, I want you to know that I am in back of you 100 per cent in your stand on this crisis. I feel like you are acting like an American and you can count on me telling other people that I feel this way.

Did you know?

You can watch a clip of Nixon making the speech in Source D on YouTube. Search for 'Nixon 3 November 1969'.

Activities

11. Consider the words Nixon used to describe the demonstrators in his speech of 3 November. What impression does he give of the anti-war movement?
12. Study Source E. Why do you think Nixon quoted this particular letter? ('I am in back of you' means 'I back you up'.)

Source F: Nixon explaining policy in Vietnam during a TV broadcast in April 1970.

Opinion polls

On 15 November 1969, 500,000 people demonstrated against the war in Washington DC. But the president felt confident that the overwhelming majority of the American people supported him and he dismissed the demonstration as irrelevant. Was he right?

Source G: Richard Nixon's approval ratings on handling of the Vietnam War, data from *The Gallup Poll 2004: Public Opinion* by George H. Gallup.

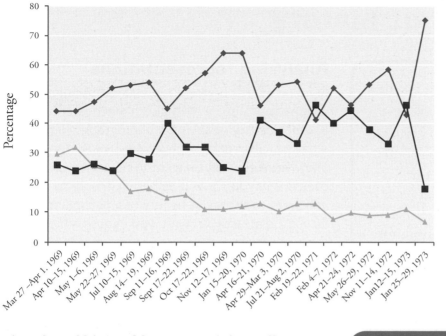

Nixon based his confidence on opinion polls. The polling organisation Gallup regularly did a national poll on the president's handling of the Vietnam War. You can see data from these polls in Source G.

While Nixon might have been pleased with his approval ratings in November 1969, Source G shows that opposition to the way the war was handled increased from 1970 through to the middle of January 1973. You can see that when the US pulled out of Vietnam at the end of January 1973, the polls showed a great surge in approval.

There are two things to remember about people's reactions to the war: there were lots of different reactions, and, as the war continued, many people's reactions also changed over time.

Activities

13. Do the data in Source G support or undermine Nixon's claims about a 'silent majority' who supported his handling of the war?

14. Approval dipped and disapproval rose at four main points in Nixon's presidency. Why do you think these events had these impacts?
    - September 1969: My Lai case brought to trial
    - April 1970: incursion into Cambodia
    - February 1971: incursion into Laos
    - April 1972: massive escalation of US bombing in North Vietnam

15. What are Source G's strengths and weaknesses in helping us decide how Americans reacted to the Vietnam War?

Summary

- There were many different opinions about the war. This means evidence needs to be investigated to find out which point of view it shows.
- It is difficult to obtain evidence about the 'silent majority'.
- People could have several different reactions, for example they might have approved of a president's handling of the war, but still wanted the war to end.
- People's reactions changed over time.

Understanding and analysing representations of history

Learning outcomes

By the end of this topic, you should be able to:

- understand what is meant by representations of history
- understand how historical representations are created
- analyse representations and judge how far they differ from one another.

What are representations of history?

A representation of history is a depiction of the past created visually or in words. It is designed to create an image of things in the past – an event, a movement, the role of an individual, and so on. Historians create representations when they write about the past. They create a picture of what life was like, why people acted as they did and what the consequences of events and developments were. Novelists, filmmakers and cartoonists also give us an image of past societies and events. In each case, the way they show their subject creates a representation of it.

Analysing representations

Someone who creates a representation takes some of the same steps you might take when creating a Facebook entry or taking a photograph. You choose what you are taking a photograph of or how to show yourself. Do you want to record an important event? Will you show it as happy or solemn? Do you want to show the beauty of a particular place? To get the effect you want, you choose which things to focus on. Sometimes you decide to leave things out. You make decisions about how to show the scene or the event.

When you analyse a representation you should look at each part separately and think about how it affects the overall image. From the details you can infer (work out) what impression the artist or author is trying to give.

A modern example of a representation

Let's first take a modern image and use the same skills needed to analyse a historical representation. Study Source A below.

Source A: An illustration from the website of the British Tourist Board, 2009. It shows a scene on the east coast of England.

| Inclusion of the boat and the windmill. | Blue sky: would the photograph have been taken on a rainy day? | Uncrowded scene: no objects in the centre of the picture. | Happy-looking young couple: do people look happy all the time? Why has the photographer not shown just one person alone? |

Note the details the photographer has chosen to include. Why have these details been included? What messages are they designed to give? Can you suggest anything which may have been deliberately left out? What do you think is the purpose of the representation in Source A?

Now study Source B. It is a photograph taken in the middle of an August morning. It shows a part of the coast near to the place shown in Source A. The building in the background is a nuclear power station.

Source B: A holiday photograph taken at Sizewell on the Suffolk coast, August 2009.

Which parts of Source A are supported by details in Source B? Would you use Source B to advertise holidays on the Suffolk coast? If not, why not? If yes, which parts of the photograph would you select?

Source A is not inaccurate, but Source B helps to show us that Source A is not a complete representation. Source A is one view and, when we analyse it, we can infer the message and purpose of this representation from the choices the photographer has made. Source A is designed to portray the coast as attractive and uncrowded, a place to enjoy walks and be happy. Its purpose is to encourage people to take holidays in the area.

Activity

1. Describe the representation of the east coast of England given in Source A. Use details from Source A. You could begin: 'Source A is a representation of the east coast. It is designed to portray it as … We can tell this because …'

   Try to use most of the following words and phrases in your description (you can use them in any order):

   - selected
   - chosen to
   - omitted
   - deliberately
   - highlighted
   - included
   - incomplete.

   You can also use details from Source B if you wish.

A case study in historical representations: the Kent State shootings

The historical context

In April 1970, President Nixon announced that US troops were assisting with a massive South Vietnamese invasion into Cambodia. Rather than finding a way to pull US troops out of Vietnam, Nixon appeared to be escalating the war.

There were anti-war demonstrations across the country, including at Kent State University in Ohio in May 1970. Rallies on Friday 1 May turned into a demonstration in the evening in the town of Kent, in which some properties were attacked and damaged. The mayor called a state of emergency, the Reserve Officers' Training Corps building was burned down and the National Guard was called in. On Monday 4 May another anti-war rally was called on the university grounds, which ended with four students being shot dead by the National Guard.

The Kent State shootings were headline news across the world. In the USA there was widespread shock and disbelief. How could American students be involved in violent protest and rioting? How could the National Guard, defenders of the American people, end up shooting college kids?

Analysing written historical representations

Analysing written representations uses the same skills you developed on pages 60–61. You note what the author has chosen to focus on, what has been included, what has been omitted, and how words are used to build up an impression.

Source C: *The New York Times* reports the shootings on 4 May 1970 (late edition).

> When the firing stopped, a slim girl, wearing a cowboy shirt and faded jeans, was lying face down on the road at the edge of the parking lot, blood pouring out onto the macadam, about 10 feet from this reporter.
>
> The youth stood stunned, many of them clustered in small groups staring at the bodies. A young man cradled one of the bleeding forms in his arms. Several girls began to cry. But many of the students who rushed from the scene seemed almost too shocked to react. Several gathered around an abstract steel sculpture in front of the building and looked at the .30-caliber bullet hole drilled through one of the plates.

Activities

2. Read the description of the shootings in Source C. How does the author portray the shock of May 4, 1970? Think about:
   - ways in which the author contrasts everyday details with shocking details
   - the impact of words like pouring, stunned, staring, cradled and drilled.

3. Why do you think the journalist chose to include the detail about the bullet hole in the sculpture? Choose from the following starters to build up your own answer to this question.
   - To make the students look foolish – they couldn't work out what had happened …
   - To prove that it was the National Guard who had fired: they had .30-calibre rifles …
   - To suggest the extreme violence used – these bullets went through *steel plates* …
   - To portray the shock the students felt …

4. Describe the representation of the Kent State shootings given in Source C. Use details from the source. You could begin 'Source C is a representation of the Kent State shootings. It is designed to portray it as … We can tell this because …' Use your answers from questions 1 and 2 to help you construct your description.

Analysing the views of historians

The views of historians are also representations. Historians aim to create an accurate representation of the past that they have researched. The views of historians may differ because they're looking *at* or looking *for* different things, or because they interpret the evidence differently.

Historians are not usually wrong or inaccurate when they differ, but they may have looked at the topic from a different perspective. Just as when people in a house look out of different windows, or look into the distance or close to the house, their different *focus* will give them a different view of the scenery. Keep this idea of *focus* in mind when you look at differences in the representations of historians. Let's look at two examples.

Source D: An extract from *The Pictorial History of the Vietnam War*, Jeremy Barnes, 1988.

> Within a week [of May 4 1970], 200 colleges and universities closed in protest strikes, many involving violent demonstrations. Washington was practically buried under mail condemning the Cambodian invasion and the tragic events at Kent State. In the face of this explosion of rage and death, Nixon was defiant...

Source E: Extracts from *Nixonland: The Rise of a President and the Fracturing of America*, Rick Perlstein, 2008.

> 'Anyone who appears on the streets of a city like Kent with long hair, dirty clothes, or barefooted deserves to be shot,' a Kent resident told a researcher.
>
> 'Have I your permission to quote that?'
>
> 'You sure do. It would have been better if the Guard had shot the whole lot of them that morning...'
>
> Much of non-student America decided the students had it coming.

These sources come from books. Sometimes, the titles can give you valuable clues about representations. The title of Source D shows that this is an illustrated history of the Vietnam War. This suggests it was probably written for people interested in finding out about the Vietnam War.

The title of Source E, which includes the word 'fracturing', suggests the author is making a particular argument: that America was divided and that this happened during Nixon's rise to power.

In Source D, Barnes describes the main events at a national level. He chooses to use words and gives details (highlighted green) to show the amount of protest there was in the USA after the Kent State shootings. The phrases highlighted in pink create the impression that many people were horrified by what happened at Kent State.

In Source E, Perlstein quotes one Kent resident's (highlighted green) reaction to the shootings. The phrases he has included (highlighted in pink) create the impression that this man was not horrified by the shootings. Perlstein uses the quote from this man to back up his argument about reactions in the USA to the shootings.

The two historians are making different points. Barnes claims Nixon was defiant (highlighted blue) despite the amount of protest. Perlstein argues (highlighted blue) that most of 'non-student America' backed Nixon against the protestors.

Activity

5. Study Sources D and E. They are both written by historians. Which four of the following statements are correct?

   - The historians disagree.
   - The historians do not actually disagree.
   - The historians are writing about different things.
   - One historian describes the reaction of many people in the US as being strongly against the Kent State shootings.
   - One historian suggests that much of 'non-student America' were not strongly against the Kent State shootings.
   - The historians' views about reactions to the protests are both accurate.

Analysing images as representations

Source F: 'Backpacking', Edd Uluschak, published in the *Edmonton Journal* (a Canadian newspaper) 20 May, 1970.

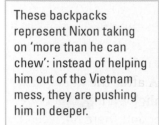

These backpacks represent Nixon taking on 'more than he can chew': instead of helping him out of the Vietnam mess, they are pushing him in deeper.

Nixon has a very worried expression: his expedition is not going according to plan.

Nixon is dressed as a typical US soldier in Vietnam.

Vietnam is shown as the biggest, heaviest-looking backpack. This shows that Nixon was deep in the swamp even before he added Cambodia and Laos to his 'load'.

Americans saw Vietnam and its neighbouring countries as hostile, alien environments – a jungle.

This swamp represents Nixon getting more and more bogged down in the war – it also reflects the sorts of conditions US troops actually experienced in Vietnam.

Source G is a famous photo of the moment after Kent State student Jeffrey Miller was shot and killed by a National Guardsman. A 14-year-old girl, Mary Ann Vecchio, is calling out in horror as she kneels beside his body. The photo was taken by a student photographer, John Filo.

Source G: John Filo's Pulitzer Prize-winning photo of the Kent State shootings.

Context for Source F

President Nixon ordered attacks into the neighbouring countries of Cambodia and Laos to wipe out North Vietnamese camps there (page 42).

Many Americans criticised this expansion of the war (page 62). Nixon had promised 'peace with honor', not more war.

Activity

6. Describe how the cartoonist of Source F has chosen to represent Nixon's decision to attack in Cambodia and Laos. Focus on details and explain why they have been included.

Source H: A drawing by artist Mark Vallen, entitled 'America is Dead'. The artist was 17 at the time of the Kent State shootings and had heard the news on the radio.

Source I: Extract from Mark Vallen's 'Art for a Change' blog

I was blinded by tears of rage and sorrow listening to that broadcast, the war had indeed 'come home' for US citizens – only now the blood of peace activists and students flowed in the streets. Though I was far away from the mayhem and bloodshed at Kent, those shootings affected me deeply, and that week I created a number of pen and ink drawings in the sketch book I always carried with me. My fury over the war poured out onto those pages ... The drawing depicts the shock and horror that was Kent State, with the sketch inspired by newspaper photographs.

Activities

7. John Filo's photo (Source G) has been reproduced in many ways for different purposes; try searching online for 'Kent State shootings – New York Times' or doing an image search for 'Kent State protest poster' to find examples of how the image has been used. Why do you think so many representations of student protest against the Vietnam War chose to use this image?

8. Compare Vallen's drawing (Source H) with Source G. What has he included from the photo in his drawing? What has he left out?

9. Vallen called his picture 'America is Dead'. Why do you think he chose that title? Use source I to help you with your answer.

10. Describe the impression Vallen creates in this picture. Use as wide a range of descriptive words as you can, for example: dramatic, stark, dark, shocking.

Comparing representations

Sources J and K are both representations of clashes between those who were protesting against the war in Vietnam and those who supported it.

Source J: Cartoon by Nicholas Garland from the *Daily Telegraph*, 15 October 1969. The cartoon shows President Nixon saying to the crowd of protesters, 'No irresponsible demonstrators are going to tell me how to run the United States!'

"No irresponsible demonstrators are going to tell me how to run the United States!"

Source K: Cartoon by Garry Trudeau from 28 December 1970.

Summary

- Representations are created to give an impression of an aspect of the past.
- The impression is created by what is included, and by the way details are drawn or by the words used.
- Historians' interpretations are also representations of the past. They sometimes differ because of the historians' focus.

Activities

11. Analyse Sources J and K. When analysing representations, first identify the big point or points the representation puts forward.

    - President Nixon made out it was only 'irresponsible', un-American hippies who were protesting against the war. How does Source J challenge this view?

    - Source K suggests that the older generation refused to listen to young people's concerns about the war. How does it do that?

12. Compare the sources carefully: a table could help with this. In the first column put specific points you want to check. In the second column add anything from the other source which supports or challenges this point. Consider how each cartoonist uses details to explain the point they are making (e.g. the flag and uniform in Source K shows the father thinks the USA is always right).

13. Reach a conclusion about 'how far'. Decide how much the differences you have found actually matter. Are they small differences, such as a matter of detail, or big differences about the main points of the representation? How much agreement is there? Weigh up the similarities and differences to decide how far they differ.

Evaluating representations

When you are evaluating a representation, you are deciding how good it is. When you evaluate anything in everyday life – what clothes to buy, for example – you use criteria. Does it fit? Is it in fashion? Is it too expensive? Is the colour right for me? You also make some criteria more important than others. If something doesn't fit, you won't buy it, even if the colour is right.

You will also use criteria when you weigh up representations of history. But let's work on an everyday example first, and then you can apply your skills to evaluating historical representations.

Activities

1. Identify three criteria you use when you decide what to eat.

2. With a partner pick a film or TV drama you have both seen.

   a. Choose three criteria by which to evaluate it, for example 'humour' or 'action-packed content'.

   b. Give the programme or film a rating of 1 to 3 against each of the criteria, and discuss your rating with your partner. You do not need to agree, but you should each be able to back up the rating you give. Refer specifically to the film or drama.

   c. Give the programme or film an overall star rating of 1 to 5. Make a display to explain your overall evaluation to your class, making sure you refer to the criteria you have used. Was one criterion so important that it had the most influence on your overall rating?

Using criteria to evaluate representations of history

There are many different kinds of representations. You could be judging between an extract from a history book, a cartoon, a work of historical fiction or a film portrayal of an event in the past. Apply criteria to each of them to make your

judgement. But remember, in order to weigh up a historical representation you must first have good knowledge of the issue which is being represented.

Using your knowledge, you can apply these tests to a representation.

- Is it accurate? Test the representation against what you know. Is it correct?

- Is it complete? Does your knowledge suggest important aspects are missing?

- Is it objective? Analyse the representation to see whether it is fair or unbalanced in its treatment. Here you could also think about the purpose of the author or artist.

The Vietnam Veterans Memorial

These sorts of questions were very important when a Vietnam veterans memorial was being planned. The war had torn America apart – how could one memorial take into account such different views? The designer had to make sure their memorial honoured those who had died for their country. But at the same time it could not glorify such an unpopular, divisive war.

Source A: The Vietnam Veterans Memorial, where the names of those who died in the war are carved into highly polished, reflective black stone.

The organisers of the Vietnam memorial wanted the design to avoid making any comment on the war at all: just to stand as a memorial for those who died. They held a competition. Source B is part of the winning entry.

Source B: Extract from Maya Lin's description of her design for the Vietnam Veterans Memorial.

> Walking through this park-like area, the memorial appears as a rift [gap] in the earth, a long, polished black stone wall, emerging from and receding into the earth ... Walking into the grassy site contained by the walls of the memorial we can barely make out the carved names upon the memorial's walls. The names, seemingly infinite in number, convey the sense of overwhelming numbers, while unifying these individuals into a whole. For this memorial is meant not as a monument to the individual, but rather as a memorial to the men and women who died during this war, as a whole.

Source C: *The Three Servicemen* statue by Frederick E. Hart.

The Vietnam Veterans Memorial is now a highly respected monument and is visited by millions each year, but it was very controversial to begin with. Some veterans, in particular, felt they were being 'buried again' in a 'black gash of shame' and there were calls for something less abstract, more heroic, more lifelike. The result was that a statue was added to the memorial site (see Source C).

Activities

3. Evaluate the memorial wall (Sources A and B) as a representation of the Vietnam conflict.
    - How did Maya Lin try to make it accurate?
    - How did she create emotional impact?
    - Was she objective: can her representation reflect different views of the war?
    - Why did some people feel her representation was not complete?

4. Now analyse Frederick Hart's representation: *The Three Servicemen* (Sources C and D). What impression is Frederick Hart trying to create with *The Three Servicemen*? Describe:
    - expressions
    - how the figures are standing
    - different races included.

5. Was adding *The Three Servicemen* necessary to complete the memorial? What do you think it adds to the memorial – or takes away?

6. How successful do you think the memorial is as a representation of how people in the USA feel about the Vietnam War?

Source D: Detail from *The Three Servicemen* statue.

Evaluating representations created by historians

Historians aim to give you their view of past events. The details in their writings are likely to be accurate. But you will still need to think about whether the view they give is the best one, depending on what you want to find out. If you want a detailed view of a period in depth, then a historian looking at overviews is not the best one for you.

Look back at the Activity on page 63. You saw that what shapes a historian's work is what the historian wants to explore and what he or she is choosing to focus on.

Detailed View **Overview**

How effective was the anti-war movement?

Study Sources E and F, thinking about the historian's focus. Even if two historians are both looking in depth or overview, they can still be looking for different things and so they have a different view. When you analyse and evaluate historians' representations, think about:

- the historian's focus
- the historian's view.

ResultsPlus
Top Tip

Students who apply criteria when evaluating representations will do well in Part B(ii) of their controlled assessment.

Source E: From *Method and Meaning in Polls and Surveys* by Howard Schuman, 2008. This is a book about opinion polls and is by a professor of sociology at a university in the USA.

> The main implication of the differences between the general public and the students is that during the Vietnam period the president had little to fear from the college anti-war movement, because the latter did not speak the same language as the larger population. Public disillusionment with the war grew despite the campus demonstrations, not because of them. The president's primary enemies were the Viet Cong and the North Vietnamese, because it was their resilience and apparent successes that undermined public support for the war. The anti-war movement was not wholly ineffective: it influenced commentators and columnists, who in turn (but in different words) affected the public.

Source F: From Melvin Small 'The Impact of the Anti-war Movement' in *Major Problems in the History of the Vietnam War*, ed. R.J. McMahon, 1995. Small is a history professor at a university in the USA.

> Anti-war activities helped convince more and more Americans to oppose the war, or at least begin to feel uncomfortable about the nation's involvement in Vietnam. Overall ... the [anti-war] movement [wore away] support for Johnson and Nixon, especially among college students at the best universities, their parents, and [well-educated people generally]. Some groups of people in the United States count for more than others ... Experts in the [anti-war] movement, the media, and on the campuses helped to destroy the knee-jerk [idea] that 'they in Washington know [what they are doing]'. This was a very important development. For the first time since 1945 ... many citizens [began] to question the judgement and wisdom of their presidents.

Activities

7. Copy this chart and complete it for Sources E and F, using as many of statements A–H as you choose. Write a statement in both columns if you think it belongs in both.

Schuman	Small
Notes for my overall evaluation of the representations	

A. The author is a respected academic who can write with authority.

B. The author is a historian writing his answer to a particular historical question.

C. The author's focus in this extract is on attitudes to the war among an important group of people.

D. The author's focus in this extract is on attitudes to the war among the general public.

E. The author's view is that the anti-war movement wore down support for the war among the most influential people in US society.

F. The author's view is that when the general public opposed the war it was for different reasons – it was not because of the anti-war movement.

G. This is a useful representation for an enquiry on the effectiveness of the anti-war movement because …

H. This representation does not include …

8. Create a context box (see page 64) for these representations (Sources E and F). Add detail on:

   • what opinion polls during the Vietnam War period showed about how people in the US reacted to the war

   • President Johnson's use of bombing against North Vietnam

   • the anti-war movement, its methods and how it was organised.

   You can add more points to your context box if you wish.

9. Which of the sources is the better representation of the effectiveness of the anti-war movement? Produce a short oral statement or a PowerPoint presentation (to last about half a minute) to evaluate both representations, and give your judgement about which you think is better. Make your criteria clear. It will help if you use the vocabulary suggested on page 61.

ResultsPlus
Top Tip

Remember, two people can come to different judgements about which representation is better and still get the same marks. The important thing is to be able to show that you have used criteria and can back up your decisions using the representations themselves and your own knowledge.

Schuman and Small are both writing accurately, but they give us different views about the anti-war movement and public opinion. How can they have different views and yet both be accurate? They can because their focus is different.

Schuman says the anti-war movement made very little connection with most people in the USA. His focus is on opinion poll data showing that most people opposed the war because America seemed to be losing. These people often did not agree with the arguments of the anti-war movement.

Small focuses on a specific group of people. He argues that the anti-war movement changed the minds of key people in US society. These key people then influenced the general public through the media. The key change was that people lost some trust in their leaders.

Another criterion to use when you are analysing historical representations is objectivity: why are writers choosing to make this representation this way? Sources G and H show two very different opinions.

Source G: From *Ending the Vietnam War*, by Henry Kissinger, 2003. Henry Kissinger was President Nixon's Secretary of State. In this extract he claims that the protestors simply blamed Nixon without suggesting any other way of handling the war which would have worked. Note: 'capitulation' means giving in (to North Vietnam).

> Extraordinarily enough, all groups, dissenters and others, passed the buck to the presidency … The practical consequence was that in the absence of any serious alternative the government was left with only its own policy or capitulation.

Source H: From *Confronting the War Machine: Draft Resistance during the Vietnam War*, by Michael S. Foley, 2003. In this extract, Foley, a US history professor, explains why he wrote his book about those who fought against the draft for the Vietnam War. He sees draft resistance as a very important form of opposition to the war and compares this to the people who fought for civil rights in the US.

> Draft resistance movement [was] the leading edge of opposition to the war in 1967 and 1968. Draft resisters were the anti-war movement's equivalent to the civil rights movement's Freedom Riders and lunch-counter sit-in participants; today, Americans regard those dissenters as heroes while they view draft resisters as selfish, cowardly, and traitorous.

Activity

Controlled assessment practice

12. Complete questions B (i) and (ii) below. Then turn to Maximise your marks, page 75, to see if you need to improve your answer.

    B (i) Study Sources E and F on page 69. They are both representations of opposition to the Vietnam War. How far do these representations differ?

    B (ii) Study Sources E and F again and Source H. Choose the one which you think is the best representation of the way in which people in the USA reacted to the Vietnam War. Explain your choice. You should use all three representations and your own knowledge to explain your answer.

Fact file

In Vietnam they call the Vietnam War 'the American War'. How do you think this war is represented in Vietnam today?

Activities

10. Kissinger was responsible for the way America got out of the war in Vietnam. He wrote his book to explain his side of the story. How does he criticise those who opposed the war in Source G? And why does this criticism make him look better?

11. Michael Foley sets out a strongly worded argument in Source H. How might evidence of very strong feelings or passionate beliefs affect the way you analyse a representation?

Summary

- A historian's writing will usually be accurate and well researched.
- Criteria must always be used when evaluating representations.
- The criteria could be: the accuracy, comprehensiveness, objectivity and purpose or focus of the representation.
- Representations must be evaluated in their historical context.

ResultsPlus
Maximise your marks

Part A Carry out a historical enquiry

In this task, you are required to carry out an enquiry; the enquiry focus will be set by Edexcel. The task is worth 20 marks and you should aim to spend about an hour writing it up. The mark scheme below shows how your teacher will mark your work for this task. Remember that in this task you are also assessed on the quality of your written communication: use historical terminology where appropriate, organise the information clearly and coherently, and make sure your spelling, punctuation and grammar are accurate.

Level	Answers at this level...	Marks available
Level 1	Make simple comments. There are few links between them and few details are given. Only one or two sources have been used in the enquiry.	1–5 marks
Level 2	Make statements about the enquiry topic. Information is included that is mostly relevant and accurate, but it is not well organised to focus on the point of the enquiry. A range of sources has been consulted and information taken from them.	6–10 marks
Level 3	Are organised to focus mainly on the point of the enquiry. Accurate and relevant information is given to support the points the student makes. A range of sources has been found and well-chosen material taken from them.	11–15 marks
Level 4	Focus well on the point of the enquiry. A well-supported conclusion is reached, for example about: the nature of change OR whether one factor was more important than the others OR the inter-relationship between two or more of the factors depending on the enquiry focus. A range of sources appropriate to the enquiry has been identified and material from the sources has been well deployed.	16–20 marks

Let's look at an extract from one student's response to the following enquiry:

- The reasons for increasing US involvement in Vietnam from 1954 to 1964

Student's answer

The period of 1954 to 1964. This was after the French were defeated in Vietnam. France was defeated in WW2 and the Japanese took over Vietnam. Ho Chi Minh fought them and then fought the French. In 1945 they came back wanting to rule Vietnam again. However, Ho had not fought the Japanese only then to hand over power to the French. The US liked Ho then and supported his fight against the French. But when the Communists took over in China and began to give help to Ho Chi Minh. Now the Americans was worried. They feared a Communist plan to dominate all of south-eat Asia. The USA poured $500 million a year into the French war effort and helped the French to set up a non-Communist government in the south of the country. But in 1954 the French was beaten again at Dien Bien Phu. That is what happened before 1954 and in 1954 then the USA was worried even more. They believed in the Domino Theory. The Domino Theory was the reason the US got involved in Vietnam but it was wrong because it never happened. After 1954 the US helped the South Vietnam government with money even though they were not a good government and the South Vietnam people didn't like them.

The Viet Cong also were a problem. They started a gerrilla war against the South Vietnamese government. Using the Ho Chi Minh trail (see Source 31). President Kennedy who was assassinated later send military advisers to fight the Viet Cong. Even though they were soldiers he called them advisers so that the US wouldn't get in trouble for fighting in Vietnam. Kennedy did not want America to get into a big war. He went step by step and maybe would have pulled out of Vietnam. His successor, Lynden Johnson, was more prepared than Kennedy to commit the USA to a full-scale conflict in Vietnam to present the spread of Communism (Walsh). In 1964 there was an attack on US ships in the Gulf of Tongking, or the US said there was anyway. It was a turning point. And so there was an excuse or a reason to get more involved. And that is what the US did, even though loads of people in the US thought Americans should not be dying to protect a country most of them had never even heard of.

Moderator's comment

This extract indicates that the response would gain a mark in level 2.

The student does make statements that link to the enquiry topic. Most of the key reasons for increased US involvement are listed. Comments are made that explain why some of these reasons were significant – the USA 'feared a Communist plan to dominate all of south-east Asia', the USA started to be involved militarily via advisers following the start of the Viet Cong's attacks in the south, President Kennedy's fears of over-commitment led to his 'step by step' approach, which is contrasted with President Johnson's bolder approach and the Gulf of Tonkin incident is described as a turning point and some explanation is given of the controversy over how justified the incident was as a reason for a massive increase in involvement.

However, there are problems: the student starts with discussion of events before 1954, which the enquiry question does not ask for, and although sources are used, the student only references the source once: Ben Walsh's *GCSE Modern World History*. This is a very well-known textbook and it is obvious that the student has copied chunks of text out of this book without referencing them. The sources are not well integrated into the student's answer and it does not look like the student has been very careful about using them: some have spelling mistakes in them, others do not fit the sense of the sentence and there is one point where the student has copied out the phrase '(see Source 31)' from the book even though there is no Source 31 in the answer. This means that the student cannot be given high marks in level 2 for quality of written communication.

To improve the response, the student should focus more centrally on the precise enquiry by looking at:

- just the period asked for in the enquiry
- which reasons the enquiry has identified for increased US involvement
- whether there is any disagreement over reasons
- which reasons the student thinks are most significant.

Additionally, the material should be better organised in the student's own words rather than simply joined together from notes.

ResultsPlus

Maximise your marks

Extract from student's improved answer

The USA's involvement in Vietnam had a long build up. Starting with the defeat of the French by Ho Chi Minh's forces in 1954, the US government tied itself to supporting the South Vietnamese against the North Vietnamese. The USA did this even though they had supported Ho Chi Minh as a freedom fighter. They did it after Communist China started to support Ho Chi Minh. The underlying reason behind all US involvement in Vietnam was fear of a Communist takeover of south-east Asia: the Domino Theory (Walsh)...
US involvement in Vietnam grew step by step. First there was what Wiest and other historians call the 'undeclared war'. The South Vietnamese government was a bad government. It was corrupt and it killed its own people for religious reasons. But the USA still supported it with money because it wasn't Communist. When the Viet Cong started a guerrilla war in South Vietnam, President Kennedy sent military 'advisers' to help fight against them. This was an important increase in involvement. Kennedy called the soldiers 'advisers' because he didn't want to get into trouble with opinion at home or internationally. And he didn't want the USA to get in too deep in Vietnam...

As Walsh says, Lyndon Johnson, was 'more prepared than Kennedy to commit the USA to a full-scale conflict in Vietnam to prevent the spread of Communism'. Historians do not all agree on why Johnson increased US involvement in this way. He had big changes he wanted to make in America, so maybe he just wanted Vietnam done with and finished so he could get on with those big changes. He also hated Communism. So the reasons here are a bit unclear. But one thing is clear: Johnson used the Gulf of Tonkin incident as his reason for increased involvement. He said North Vietnam had made an unprovoked attack on the USA, and the US government was very happy to give the president all the powers and money he needed to escalate the war to first large-scale bombing and then, when that didn't work (Carrington), to sending in the troops.

So, although generally the USA went step by step into the Vietnam War, underneath it all was the Domino Theory and that is what I think was the most important reason.

ResultsPlus
Maximise your marks

Part B(i) Compare two representations

In this task, you are required to analyse and compare two representations of history. The task is worth 10 marks and you should aim to spend about 30 minutes writing it up. The mark scheme below shows how your teacher will mark your work for this task.

Level	Answers at this level…	Marks available
Level 1	Show an understanding of the main features of the two representations and select material from them. The responses are descriptions, direct quotations or paraphrases from one or more of the sources.	1–3 marks
Level 2	Show an understanding of the two representations and select similarities and/or differences of detail from them. At low level 2, there may be only one developed comparison, and other comparisons will be undeveloped or unsupported with material from the sources.	4–7 marks
Level 3	Analyse the representations and identify a range of similarities and/or differences in representation. Then use precisely selected detail from the two representations to support the explanation and make a judgement about extent.	8–10 marks

Let's look at an extract from one student's response to the representations below.

- Study Representations E and F from page 69. They are both representations of the way in which people in the USA reacted to the Vietnam War. How far do these representations differ? (10 marks)

Student's answer

Representation E and Representation F are both about the anti-war movement and reactions to the Vietnam War. Representation E describes how most people in the US didn't agree with the anti-war movement. Instead most people reacted against the war when they thought they weren't winning against the Viet Cong and North Vietnamese. But Representation F does not agree. It says the anti-war movement did make more and more people oppose the war. Also, Representation E is written by a sociologist and Representation F is by a historian. So overall they differ quite a bit, though Representation F does talk about 'many citizens began to question', which links with Representation E.

ResultsPlus
Maximise your marks

Moderator comment

In this part of the answer, the student understands some of the details in the representations and does compare them. We can see the language of comparison is used: 'Both about', 'does not agree', 'differ quite a bit'.

The student has pointed out the key difference between the representations: one arguing there was no connection between the anti-war movement and other US opposition to the war, the other claiming that the anti-war movement did have a significant impact on the wider population. A similarity is noted with the reference to 'began to question', but this aspect should have been further developed.

There is enough comprehension and comparison for the answer to get into level 2, but the answer concentrates mainly on differences in content in the two representations. To raise the response to the next level, the answer should show more awareness of the extent to which there are differences in the portrayal of the influence of the anti-war movement. A key distinction here could be the author's focus. Representation E is dealing with opinion poll evidence and looking at the attitudes in the whole population – the general public. Representation F's focus is on the influence of the anti-war movement on an influential group of people. The focus of the two representations alters their portrayals of the influence of the anti-war movement.

Extract from student's improved answer

Representation E and Representation F are both about the anti-war movement and reactions to the Vietnam War. They are asking the same sort of question: how much influence did the anti-war movement have on US society and on Presidents Johnson and Nixon? They both agree too that there was a negative reaction to the war amongst the general population. This is an important aspect of both representations.

The big difference between the two Representations is their views of the influence of anti-war movement. Representation E has chosen to highlight other reasons for opposition to the war and even suggests that the anti-war movement did not influence public opinion – 'disillusionment with the war grew despite the campus demonstrations, not because of them'. Representation E emphasises that most people reacted against the war because of the 'apparent successes' of the Viet Cong and North Vietnamese. So it portrays the anti-war movement as having little influence on the general public or the president. Instead, many people reacted negatively to the war for completely different reasons. But Representation F does not agree. It says the anti-war movement did make the media and more and more people ask questions about the war. Representation F takes the view that some people are more important in society than others. The anti-war movement influenced these key people, and they influenced the rest of society.

Overall, this means the two representations are significantly different in their view of the influence of the anti-war movement on reactions in the USA – Representation E gives the impression that it had no real influence – 'the president had little to fear', Representation F gives the impression that it was important – it led 'many citizens to question the judgement of the president.'

ResultsPlus
Maximise your marks

Part B(ii) Analyse and evaluate three representations

In this task, you are required to analyse and evaluate three representations of history. The task is worth 20 marks and you should aim to spend about an hour writing it up. The mark scheme below shows how your teacher will mark your work for this task. Remember that in this task you are also assessed on the quality of your written communication: use historical terminology where appropriate, organise the information clearly and coherently, and make sure your spelling, punctuation and grammar are accurate.

Level	Answers at this level…	Marks available
Level 1	Show an understanding of the main features of the sources and select material. Simple judgements are made about the representation, and a limited amount of accurate information about the period is given. The material is mostly generalised, and links to the representation are not explicit.	1–5 marks
Level 2	Show an understanding of the main features of the three sources and select key features of the representations from them. Judgement is made about the best representation and there is detailed and accurate material about the period, but with little linkage between description and judgement. Judgements may relate to the accuracy or comprehensiveness of the representation.	6–10 marks
Level 3	Analyse the three sources and show some of the ways in which the past situation has been represented. Detail from the sources is used to support the analysis. There is a critical evaluation of the representation based on well selected information about the period and at least two clear criteria are applied, for example the author's purpose or objectivity, or the comprehensiveness and/or accuracy of the representation.	11–15 marks
Level 4	Analyse the three sources to show the way in which the past situation has been represented. Precisely selected detail from the sources is used to support the analysis. There is a critical evaluation of the representation based on precisely selected information about the period and applying at least three criteria, for example the author's purpose or objectivity, or the comprehensiveness and/or accuracy of the representation.	16–20 marks

Let's look at an extract from one student's response to the representations.

- Study Representations E and F on page 69 and Representation K on page 66. Choose the one which you think is the best representation of the way in which people in the USA reacted to the Vietnam War. Explain your choice. You should use all three representations and your own knowledge to explain your answer. (20 marks)

Student response

I think Representation K is useful because it shows there were different reactions in a family. It is not very accurate because it's only a cartoon and aims to be funny, but we do know that young people opposed the war most, so that part of it is true.

I think Representation F is not so useful because it doesn't recognise different reactions to the war. It is not comprehensive. It says the anti-war movement influenced public opinion.

I think Representation E is useful because it comes from opinion poll evidence and it gives us information about several ways people reacted to the war… Both Representations E and F are better than Representation K in saying why reactions happened. Representation E is most useful because it gives us accurate information about reactions to the war from the whole public. We know that people did demonstrate against the anti-war demonstrations and opinion polls did find out what people thought about the war.

Moderator comment

The student has made a short comment which identifies the core information which each representation can provide. The student has begun to use some criteria to evaluate the representations, but none of the comments are developed very far. The student uses the criterion of accuracy to evaluate Representation K. This is a good choice of a criterion by which to evaluate a cartoon. But the student uses only a limited amount of their own knowledge to test accuracy. To improve the answer, the student should make more use of contextual knowledge and analyse the cartoon more fully to show its accuracy.

In evaluating Representations E and F, the student has chosen a valid criterion for the best representation of the way in which people in the USA reacted to the Vietnam War – what the representations tell us about the range of ways people reacted to the war. Here the student is basing the judgement on the focus of the representations, though this should be made more explicit. However, the student's comments need to make much more use of contextual knowledge, relating the evaluation to knowledge of the way people reacted to the war.

To reach the highest level the student should use three criteria to rate each representation.

Extract from student's improved answer

I think Representation E is useful because it explains some possible reasons behind people's reactions against the war and it deals with a range of reactions. It is the most comprehensive of the three. It says 'public disillusionment with the war grew' and it explains that public support fell because of the North Vietnamese and Viet Cong 'resilience and apparent successes'. We know from opinion poll data that this is accurate. Although specific events caused ups and downs in the polls, the trend overall was a decline in the numbers approving of Nixon's handling of the war after 1969. But at the same time, in this extract, this Representation does not show that people (the silent majority) continued to support the war, even when it was not going so well, so it is not fully comprehensive.

I think representation F is not so useful because it only focuses on the influence of the anti-war movement. It shows the importance of the movement – that it had an influence on an educated group. It also implies that this group was especially important. But it does not include other groups...

Cartoons like Representation K show us general attitudes – people find them funny because there is a bit of truth in them. We do know that the anti-war movement grew strongly amongst students and that young people in the sixties were more likely to question authority... People in the older generation who had been part of the Second World War were more likely to feel patriotic.... So Representation K is accurate when it portrays different reactions between father and son in a family. But, of course, it is not an accurate representation of the attitudes in every family...

Representations E and F are both trying to be objective, their different views come from their different focus. Representation K is not trying to be objective or comprehensive. It is just making a point about the generation gap. All three representations are accurate in what they say, but they are not complete. Overall Representation E seems to be the best representation because it is the most comprehensive.

Glossary

ARVN: Army of the Republic of Vietnam – South Vietnamese Army.

Civil war: a war between different groups of people within the same state.

Cluster bombs: bombs used by the US military which released hundreds of smaller 'bomblets' over a wide area.

Communism: a system of organising society so that all property belongs to the community in general and not to individuals. Everything is controlled by the state and a single political party.

Context: the background information that helps you understand a source.

Coup: a sudden overthrow of an existing government and seizure of political power, often carried out by the army.

Guerrilla warfare: a type of warfare where a smaller, less well-supplied force uses stealth and hit-and-run tactics to fight a larger force.

Morale: the belief of a group of people in their shared aims and their ability to work together to achieve it.

Napalm: gasoline mixed with a paste of chemicals to form a jelly. When ignited, the jelly structure means the burning gasoline sticks to substances (like skin), increasing the damage done by this weapon.

NLF: National Liberation Front – North Vietnamese supporters in South Vietnam.

NVA: North Vietnamese Army.

Objective: the overall aim or goal.

Stalemate: a situation in which neither side can make progress.

Strategy: the plan of action to achieve the objective.

Tactics: the methods and activities used in the plan.

Viet Cong: the US and South Vietnamese governments' term for NLF fighters.

Vietminh: a national liberation movement formed to fight against French and Japanese control of Vietnam.

Published by Pearson Education Limited, a company incorporated in England and Wales, having its registered office at Edinburgh Gate, Harlow, Essex, CM20 2JE. Registered company number: 872828

Edexcel is a registered trademark of Edexcel Limited

Text © Pearson Education Limited

First published 2010

12 11 10
10 9 8 7 6 5 4 3 2 1

British Library Cataloguing in Publication Data
A catalogue record for this book is available from the British Library.

ISBN 978 1 846906 47 3

Designed and typeset by Juice Creative Ltd, Hertfordshire
Original illustrations © Pearson Education Ltd 2010

Printed in Great Britain at Scotprint, Haddington

Acknowledgements
We would like to thank Dr Martin Thornton for his invaluable help in the development of this material.

Picture credits
The publisher would like to thank the following for their kind permission to reproduce their photographs:

(Key: b-bottom; c-centre; l-left; r-right; t-top)

Alamy Images: nobleIMAGES 67; Corbis: 23, 28, Bettmann 20, David J. Frent 56/4, 56/5, 56/6, David J. Frent 56/4, 56/5, 56/6, David J. Frent 56/4, 56/5, 56/6, Tim Page 29; **Getty Images**: 58, Frank Barratt 39, AFP PHOTO / Karen BLEIER 68, 68/2, Patrick Christain 19, John Dominis 7, John Filo 64, Ronald L. Haeberle 34, George Silk / TIME & LIFE Images 8, Lee Lockwood / TIME & LIFE Images 2, Fred W. McDarrah 55, MPI 15; **The Picture Collection Inc.**: 30/2, Henri Huet / AP Henri Huet / AP / Press Association 30, Lee Lockwood Lee Lockwood / Getty Images 33; **Angela Leonard**: 61; **Rutland Frederick Limited**: 56, 56/2, 56/3; **National Archives and Records Administration (NARA)**: 18, 18/2; **Photolibrary.com**: Britain on View 60; **Press Association Images**: AP 12, 38, AP 12, 38, Eddie Adams / AP 41; **Rex Features**: Everett Collection 9; **U.S. Air Force Museum Photo Archives**: 13; Mark Vallen: 65/2

Cover images: Front: **Corbis**: Christian Simonpietri

All other images © Pearson Education

Every effort has been made to trace the copyright holders and we apologise in advance for any unintentional omissions. We would be pleased to insert the appropriate acknowledgement in any subsequent edition of this publication.

We are grateful to the following for permission to reproduce copyright material:

Cartoons
Cartoon on page 64 from Vietnam Cambodia Laos, by Edd Uluschak, May 20, 1970, http://edocs.lib.sfu.ca/cgi-bin/Cartoons?CartoonID=4269, copyright © Simon Fraser University; Cartoon on page 66 by Nicholas Garland from http://www.cartoons. ac.uk/record/16466, copyright (c) Telegraph Media Group Limited 1969; Cartoon on page 66 by Garry Trudeau 'Doonesbury', 28 December 1970 from http://www. amureprints.com/, Doonesbury (c) 1970 G.B. Trudeau. Reprinted by permission of Universal Uclick. All rights reserved.

Text
Extract on page 10 adapted from Vietnam, Korea and US Foreign Policy 1945-75, Heinemann (Bragg, C. 2005) p. 110, Pearson Education Ltd; Extracts on page 10, page 48, page 51 adapted from Ideology, Conflict and Retreat: The USA in Asia 1950-1973, Pearson Education Ltd. (Stewart, G. 2009); Extracts on page 10, page 48, page 51 from Ideology, Conflict and Retreat: The USA in Asia 1950-1973, Pearson Education Ltd (Stewart, G. 2009);

Extracts on page 10, page 50 adapted from GCSE Modern World History, 2nd ed., Hodder Education (Walsh, B. 2001), reproduced by permission of John Murray (Publishers) Ltd; Extract on page 20 adapted from The Vietnam War: The Story and Photographs, Brassey's Inc. (Goldstein, D. M., Dillion, K. V., Wenger, J. M. 1999), with permission from Potomac Books, Inc; Extract on page 29 adapted from Vietnam: A

war lost and won, Arcturus Publishing (Cawthorne, N. 2008) p. 203, with permission from Arcturus Publishing Ltd. and Nigel Cawthorne; Extract on page 29 from Speech by General William C. Westmoreland before the Third Annual Reunion of the Vietnam Helicopter Pilots Association (VHPA) at the Washington, DC Hilton Hotel on July 5th, 1986, reproduced in a Vietnam Helicopter Pilots Association Historical Reference Directory Volume 2A (http://www.vhfcn.org/stat.html, with permission from Vietnam Helicopter Pilots Association; Extracts on page 33, page 48 from Legacy of Discord: Voices of the Vietnam War Era, Brassey's Inc. (Dorland, G. 2001), with permission from Potomac Books, Inc; Extract on page 46 adapted from OCR GCSE History B: Modern World History Student Book, Heinemann (Carrington, E., Hill, A., Brodkin, A. and Kerridge, R. 2009) p. 81, Pearson Education Ltd; Extract on page 47 adapted from Gulf of Tonkin Incident - 1964, published 21 February 2008, http://www.workers.org/2008/world/gulf_of_tonkin_incident_0221/, Copyright (c) 2009 Workers World. Verbatim copying and distribution of articles is permitted in any medium without royalty provided this notice is preserved; Extract on page 48 from United States 1776-1992, Collins Education (Murphy, D., Cooper, K., Waldron, M. 2001) p. 298, reprinted by permission of HarperCollins Publishers Ltd. (c) 2001 D. Murphy, K. Cooper and M. Waldron; Extract on page 51 adapted from Legacy of Discord, Brassey's Inc. (Dorland, G.), with permission from Potomac Books, Inc; Extract on page 55 from text of interview with Senator John Stennis published at http://www.pbs.org/wgbh/amex/vietnam/series/pt_10.html, from WGBH-TV Boston. Copyright (c) 1996-2009 WGBH Educational Foundation; Extract on page 62 from 4 Kent State Students Killed by Troops, The New York Times, 4 May 1970 (John Kifner), from The New York Times, (c) 5/4/1970 The New York Times All rights reserved. Used by permission and protected by the Copyright Laws of the United States. The printing, copying, redistribution, or retransmission of the Material without express written permission is prohibited; Extract on page 63 reprinted with the permission of Scribner, a Division of Simon & Schuster, Inc., from Nixonland: The Rise of a President and the Fracturing of America by Rick Perlstein. Copyright (c) 2008 by Rick Perlstein. All rights reserved; Extract on page 65 from Mark Vallen's Art For A Change website, http://art-for-a-change. com/blog/2006/05/kent-state-four-dead-in-ohio.html, copyright © Mark Vallen; Extract on page 69 from Major Problems in the History of the Vietnam War, edited by R. J. McMahon, pub. D. C. Heath & Co., The Impact of the Anti-war Movement (Small, M. 1995) p. 489, with permission from Professor Melvin Small; Extract on page 71 reprinted with the permission of Simon & Schuster, Inc. from Ending the Vietnam War by Henry Kissinger. Copyright (c) 1979, 1982, 1999, 2003 by Henry A. Kissinger; Extract on page 69 from Method and Meaning in Polls and Surveys, 978-0-6740-2827-2, Harvard University Press (Howard Schuman 2008) 72, Reprinted by permission of the publisher from Method and Meaning in Polls and Surveys by Howard Schuman, Cambridge, Mass.: Harvard University Press, p.72, copyright © 2008 by President and Fellows of Harvard College; Quote on page 58 from http:// www.presidency.ucsb.edu/ws/index.php?pid=2303, John T. Woolley and Gerhard Peters, The American Presidency Project [online]. Santa Barbara, CA. Available from World Wide Web: http://www.presidency.ucsb.edu/ws/?pid=2303; Extract on page 71 from Confronting the War Machine: Draft Resistance during the Vietnam War, University of North Carolina Press (Michael S. Foley 2003), From Confronting the War Machine: Draft Resistance during the Vietnam War by Michael S. Foley. Copyright © 2003 by the University of North Carolina Press. Used by permission of the publisher. www.uncpress.unc.edu

Tables
Table on page 32 adapted from Statistics of Vietnamese Democide: Estimates, Calculations, and Sources (Rummel, R. J. 1997) http://www.hawaii.edu/powerkills, with permission from Professor Rudolph J. Rummel; Table 10.1 from Vietnam, Korea and US Foreign Policy 1945-75, Heinemann (Bragg, C. 2005) p. 158, Pearson Education Ltd; Table on page 59 from Nixon's approval ratings on handling of the Vietnam War, The Gallup Poll 2004: Public Opinion, George H. Gallup, 978074255138 p. 240

In some instances we have been unable to trace the owners of copyright material, and we would appreciate any information that would enable us to do so.

Websites
The websites used in this book were correct and up to date at the time of publication. It is essential for tutors to preview each website before using it in class so as to ensure that the URL is still accurate, relevant and appropriate. We suggest that tutors bookmark useful websites and consider enabling students to access them through the school/college intranet.

Disclaimer
This material has been published on behalf of Edexcel and offers high-quality support for the delivery of Edexcel qualifications. This does not mean that the material is essential to achieve any Edexcel qualification, nor does it mean that it is the only suitable material available to support any Edexcel qualification. Edexcel material will not be used verbatim in setting any Edexcel examination or assessment. Any resource lists produced by Edexcel shall include this and other appropriate resources.

Copies of official specifications for all Edexcel qualifications may be found on the Edexcel website: www.edexcel.com